To Darling Lolly
Merry Christmas
We love you
Kelly and Keith
XOXO
SYDNEY 2016

HEALING MEALS
for mums

Sunjoo Kim

First published by REMIPE® Pty Ltd in 2016

National Library of Australia Cataloguing-in-Publication entry:

Author: Kim, Sunjoo.
Title: Healing Meals for Mums: Family recipes and remedies to prevent and
               heal everyday illnesses / Sunjoo Kim
ISBN: 9780994320704 (paperback)
Subjects: Cooking.
               Cooking (Natural Foods).
               Mothers--Nutrition.
               Health.
Dewey Number: 641.563

Cover design and layout by Julia Kuris, www.designerbility.com.au
Photography by CreativeXposure Photography and Sunjoo Kim

Disclaimer
The material in this publication is of the nature of general comment only and does not represent professional advice. It is not intended to provide specific guidance for particular circumstances and it should not be relied on as the basis for any decision to take action on any matter which it covers. Readers should obtain professional advice where appropriate before making any such decision. To the maximum extent permitted by law, the author and publisher disclaim all responsibility and liability to any person arising directly or indirectly from any person taking or not taking action based on the information in this publication.

Dedicated...

To Leo, Julien and Pierre-Francis whom I love with all my heart.

To my late grandparents who taught me the happiness
and joy of sharing food.

And to mothers everywhere, who have the noble duty
of creating meals and sharing love every day.

About the author

Sunjoo Kim was born in Seoul, South Korea and grew up under the care of her grandparents. Her grandmother was an inspirational cook who taught Sunjoo how to prepare and enjoy traditional Korean dishes and flavours.

Growing up in Seoul, the young Sunjoo developed a very broad and sophisticated culinary appreciation of Asian cooking.

Over 15 years ago, Sunjoo fell in love with a Frenchman, Pierre-Francis, and they moved to Australia to make a life together. Sunjoo thus began her love affair with the finest of western cuisine. It is this delicious fusion of eastern and western traditions that provides the nutritional foundation and the focus on pleasure in her approach.

Sunjoo's food reflects her life experiences, as a child in her grandmother's kitchen in Korea, as a young IT professional in Lyon discovering the joys of French cuisine, and as a loving mother in Sydney preparing nutritious food for her family.

" I started writing this book when I remembered my late grandmother's love for me expressed through her food. When I was not well, my grandmother always knew what to cook to make me feel better. Food was not only fuel for everyday life, but also a medicine created with love. I hope that this book will help you enjoy the healing benefits of food as well as its pleasure and the love it delivers. "

Acknowledgements

I found that the challenges of writing a book for the first time are similar to the ones when you become a mother for the first time: You have no prior knowledge or experience, therefore it feels extra hard and you need lots of help.

I cannot thank my friends and family enough for all the support and love I received in the creation of this book.

My special thanks to…

Paula Goncalves for helping me start writing this book and encouraging me throughout with great advice.

Bronwyn Hay, Susan Bryant and Marie Gallagher for reviewing and refining this book as my first readers.

Key Person of Influence for helping me reshape this book to the next level so that I feel confident to publish.

My alumni at Key Person of Influence – Fran Connelley, Janet Smith, Craig Hooper, Lee Gabbett, Neil Campbell, Andrew Akratos, Karen Sanders and Michele Gennoe for your steadfast support, coaching, and insights you did not spare to enable me to bring this book to fruition.

Julia Kuris for your amazing design and passion to transform this book to its final form.

Leo, Julien and Pierre-Francis for trusting me and being the reason for this extraordinary journey.

Contents

Contents

Part 2: *continued...*

Basics

REMEDY
+
RECIPE
=
REMIPE®

Remipe

noun / rem.i.pi /

A recipe that is also a remedy for sickness or symptoms of illness.

Remipes are simple and quick to cook, easy to clean up afterwards, help you feel better and are yummy to eat.

Example:

For your nasty cold, try these remipes to recover quickly.

Do you know a good remipe to ease the gastro my child is suffering from?

From the Sunjoo Kim dictionary

my philosophy

I want many things…

- to eat delicious food.
- to spend a minimum amount of time, without hassle, to cook food and clean up afterwards.
- food to keep me healthy and in great shape.
- food to be an aid in healing any sickness or ailment I have.
- to know what to cook for the people I love and for myself when we're not feeling well.
- that positive energy and sense of regaining control that only comes from taking action and doing something about a problem.

I believe in the healing energy of the food we eat, and food greatly influences the way we look and feel.

Happiness can come from sharing a delicious and healthy meal with our family and this simple happiness does enormous good for our mind, our body and our wellbeing.

So, I created 'Remipes'. I've combined 'remedy' and 'recipe' to create the Remipes in this book. You can use Remipes as remedies when you are sick and also as everyday recipes to keep you well.

To get the most from every REMIPE®, here are a few important tips to keep in mind:

①

Use organic produce whenever you can. If not, find seasonal and the freshest produce you can. Remember that when the ingredients are good, you have a much better chance of the finished dish being good.

②

Remipes are intended to boost the healing process by complementing medicine. They are not intended as a substitute.

③

I've included the nutritional information in my remipes to help you understand how each remipe may assist in healing an illness.

PART 1

Stop dieting, Start living

Establishing a life-long habit of balanced eating

Let's face it, a short-term diet of any sort hardly ever works.

We exercise tremendous will power and 'fight against food' in many different ways – by limiting calories, avoiding certain types of food, only eating a 'super' food, eating more often, eating only at certain times, fasting, and the list goes on and on.

These diets are all too hard. Even if we succeed, more often than not, we regress back to where we were. Or worse, soon after coming off a diet, we go back to the same old eating and cooking habits that created the issues we had before.

The damage is not only physical but also deeply emotional. We are no longer in love with or in a peaceful relationship with food when we diet. We treat food as an object to conquer, or even as an enemy to fight in order to get into the shape or health state we desire.

I am one of those food lovers who wonder whether they eat to live or live to eat. The last thing I want is to constantly struggle with food.

I wish my parents had taught me good habits and attitudes towards food from the beginning. Wouldn't it be easier if I had learnt those things as a child rather than as an adult?

With the rising trend of serious health issues such as diabetes, high blood pressure, heart attacks and cancer, can we afford not to establish the right eating habits as early as possible in our life?

> *I want my chidren to have the pleasure of eating without guilt.*

And so I realised that if things were going to change, it was up to me. I want my children to learn how to nourish their bodies so they can live long and healthy lives. I want them to have the pleasure of eating without guilt. I know I hold the key role in forming their relationship with food from the early stage of their lives.

With this realisation, I was determined to find a new way to establish a life-long habit of balanced eating that restores my peace and love with food – not just for myself, but for my sons – and their children.

The Remipe Approach

My happiest memories as a child are from the family table: sharing delicious family meals cooked by my grandmother when I grew up in Asia. My grandmother was an inspirational cook. She also knew what to cook when I was not well based on the knowledge she had inherited from generations before her.

Whether it was science or simply because my grandmother cooked with love, I remember I always felt better after eating her food. Food was not only pleasure and fuel for my life, but also a medicine created with love.

When I became a mother, I deeply felt the desire to bring this experience back to my family. Family meals are one of the best ways to create happiness every day, not only with the sensuous pleasure of food but with the health giving benefits of preventing and healing illnesses.

Whether it was science or love, I always felt better after eating my grandmother's food.

I researched high-potency foods and the most beneficial nutrients to prevent and heal everyday illnesses. I know the challenges in everyday cooking as a mother – the lack of time, energy and creativity. So I created these simple yet exciting recipes using high potency foods with the required nutrients for specific illnesses. I call them 'Remipes', combining remedy and recipe. Remipes use common, seasonal and economic ingredients and are simple to cook, minimising the time needed to shop, cook and clean up afterwards.

Detail from Three Ages of Woman after Gustav Klimt © Fran McGarry

After the birth of my second son Leo, I experienced the worst health of my life. My first boy Julien was four and I remember at least 10 separate visits to the doctor in that year. My immunity was challenged further when the kids came home from day care and preschool with everyday illnesses. These challenges are typical for mothers. Furthermore, there's hardly any downtime for mothers with the continuing demands from their family. Mothers can't afford to be sick!

So, I confess that I created remipes for myself in the first place.

They always say when the plane takes off, in an aircraft emergency, you should put on an oxygen mask for yourself first before you help your children. I knew I had to help myself first in order to be there for my family.

You cannot expect to take advantage of the medicinal benefits of food by eating healing meals just once or twice. The key is to eat the right food on an ongoing basis, therefore the remipe approach is easy and attractive enough to be followed on a daily basis.

I had to help myself first to be there for my family.

I use my remipes for my family every day for prevention and healing of illnesses. The result is immensely rewarding:

- My family and I are healthier.
- My family love the food I cook.
- I feel great about the contribution I make to my family's health and happiness.

I have written this book to share this positive experience.

Pleasure, Healing and Love

Over 15 years ago, I met my husband, Pierre-Francis, in Lyon, France.

As a Frenchman, the first thing he suggested was that we have lunch together. I still clearly remember the beautiful sunny autumn day when we first sat together at an outdoor table of a small French restaurant on a hill.

Pierre-Francis took his time to explain the menu and regional specialties, and carefully suggested an entrée, main and dessert that I would enjoy. We ordered different food and shared everything as if we were having a degustation meal. I knew at that moment Pierre-Francis and I had something very important in common – a passion and love for food.

Yes, I like using butter and cream for their flavour, but in moderation.

I have learnt to cook and enjoy French home cooking every day. My French mother-in-law is also a great cook and she inspires me with her own recipes and her health-conscious cooking style. This has greatly influenced my balanced approach – I do not compromise the enjoyment of food simply for health benefits. I've discovered over the years that meals can be indulgent and pleasurable as well as healthy.

I disagree that one should have to choose between the pleasure of eating and the benefits of a healthy diet. I take daily inspiration from my French husband who enjoys both. I believe that we can eat everything in moderation and that every food has goodness. Yes, I like using butter and cream for their flavour, but in moderation. It is critical to have the right amount of fat for the flavour of a dish. Fat is not an obstacle for health; on the contrary, good fats are vital for our health, including maintaining beautiful skin and hair.

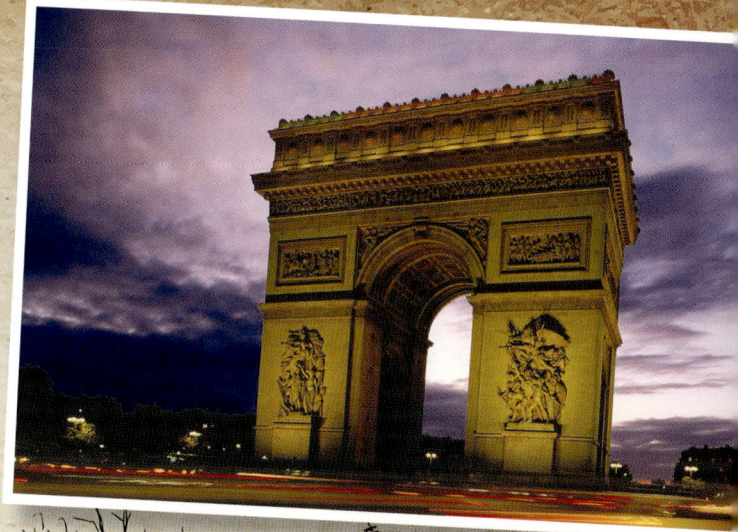

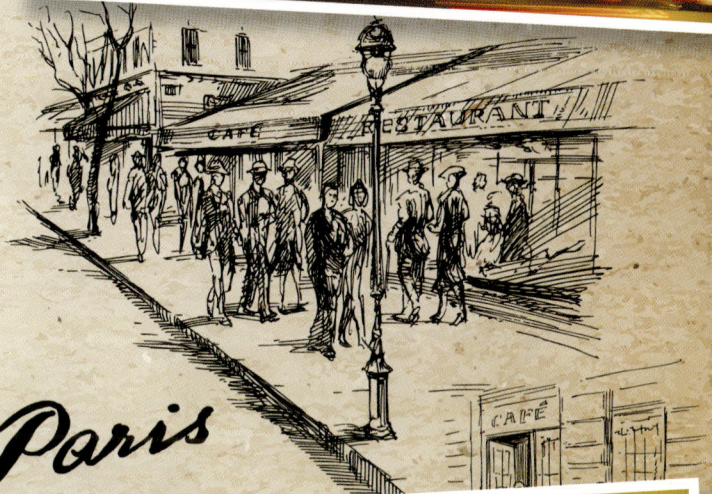

Paris

The more I research the healing benefits of food, the more evidence I find that Nature rewards our effort to have sensuous pleasure when eating with extra health benefits. For example, beta carotene in carrots (the precursor to vitamin A) is absorbed better when carrots are cooked with some fat. When you sprinkle ground cinnamon on your sweet dessert, the glycaemic index (GI) of your dessert gets lowered. I am convinced that Nature wants us to enjoy both pleasure and health.

I believe that our body naturally regulates appetite and controls the right amount of food that it requires when we eat nutritional and flavoursome food, taking our time and with a relaxed mind. I found myself wanting to eat more than I need when I am rushing to eat foods that are nutritionally poor or with commercially created tastes high in salt, sugar and (or) fat.

Trust your body's own ability to decide the optimal amount of food it needs, instead of counting calories.

Instead of trying hard to reduce the calorie intake, I suggest focusing on having nutritious and soul-satisfying food made with high-quality ingredients and care, trusting your body's self-regulatory ability for deciding the optimal amount it needs.

In my mind, there are 4 types of foods:

1. Pleasurable to eat + make you feel good afterwards
2. Pleasurable to eat + make you feel bad afterwards
3. Unpleasant to eat + make you feel bad afterwards
4. Unpleasant to eat + make you feel good afterwards

4 Types of Foods Quadrant

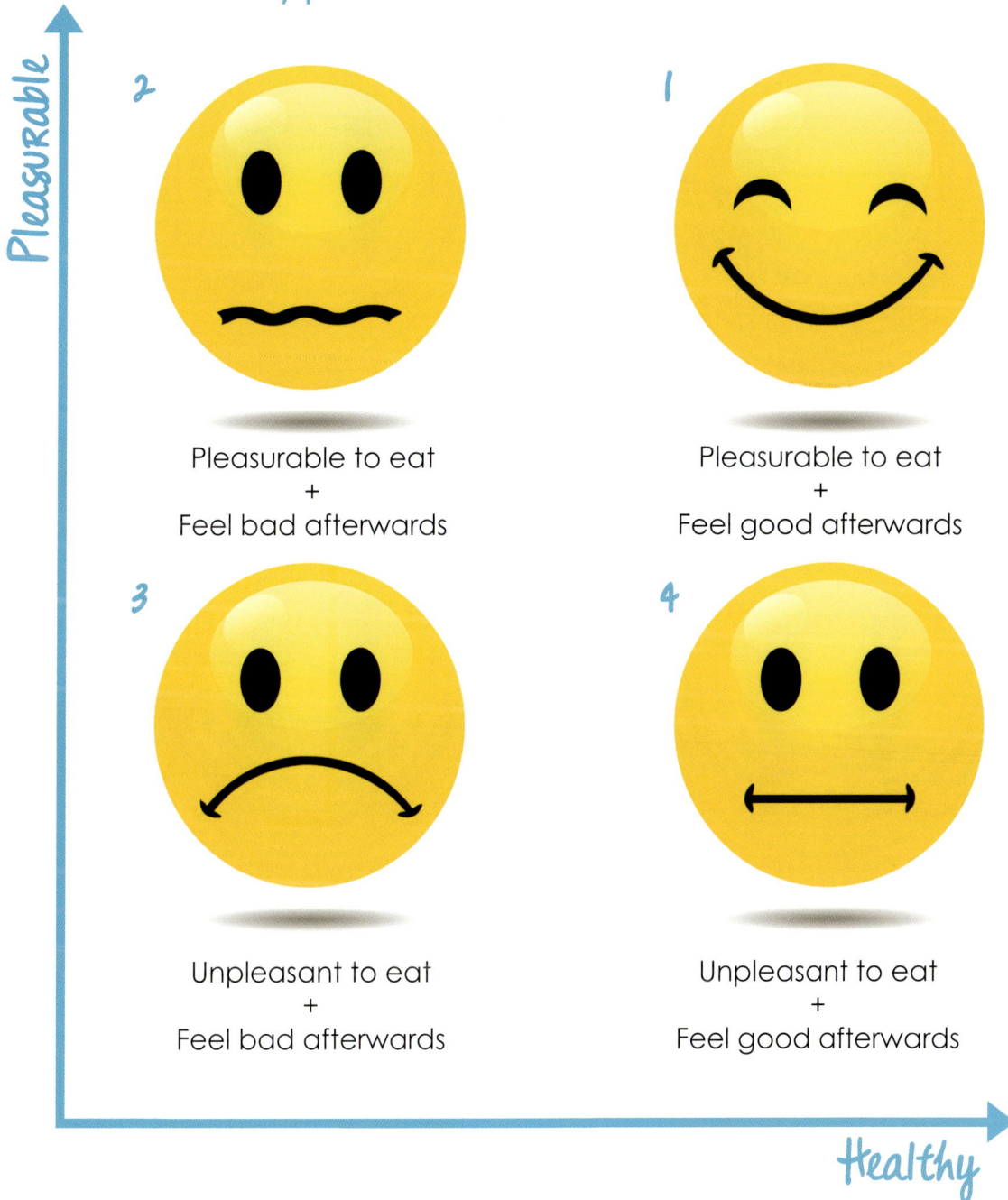

Pleasurable (vertical axis)

Healthy (horizontal axis)

2

Pleasurable to eat
+
Feel bad afterwards

1

Pleasurable to eat
+
Feel good afterwards

3

Unpleasant to eat
+
Feel bad afterwards

4

Unpleasant to eat
+
Feel good afterwards

Of course, remipes are designed to be the first type, i.e. pleasurable to eat and make you feel good afterwards with the health benefits.

We need to educate our children and ourselves about the four types of food, and form a habit of making the right food choices (well, at least most of the time).

The perception of what is 'pleasurable to eat' may change over time based on your eating habits. When you are used to enjoying meals with great flavours from fresh ingredients cooked with care, you may not be so attracted to those fast foods or takeaways with artificial tastes. Those commercial foods have no soul in them, hence they may no longer be perceived as 'pleasurable to eat'. I am convinced that this shift will happen to you on your journey with the remipe approach.

I enjoy the whole process of planning, shopping, cooking, eating and getting my kitchen ready for the next family meal, because it is through that whole process I transfer my passion and love of food to my loved ones and myself. However, I am well aware of and have experienced the difficulties of everyday cooking: lack of time, energy, information and creativity. Therefore, I have made every effort to help mothers overcome these challenges by making this book as pragmatic as possible for their daily usage.

Mothers perform the key role for the wellbeing of the current and future generations by creating a family table where love is tangibly expressed, enjoyed and shared every day.

" I dedicate this book to mothers who want to do more for their family and themselves with their limited time, energy and their UNLIMITED LOVE. "

PART 2
Remipes for...

Creamy spinach and egg pasta

serves 4

INGREDIENTS

400 g	thin spaghetti
1	tablespoons salt to cook the pasta (add when the water boils)
2	tablespoons canola oil
20 g	butter
400 g	spinach, washed and cut (or pre-washed baby spinach is handy)
5	cloves garlic, thinly sliced
2	eggs, whisked
½	teaspoon nutmeg powder
200 g	mascarpone cheese
½	cup Parmesan cheese powder
4	tablespoons dry toasted pine nuts

METHOD

Cook the pasta in a large saucepan of salted, boiling water for 10-12 minutes or until al dente.

While the pasta is cooking, heat a wok or medium frying pan over medium heat. Add the oil, butter and spinach and cook for 1 minute or until the spinach is wilted.

When the spinach turns dark green, turn the heat to low and add garlic, egg, nutmeg, mascarpone and Parmesan cheese. Cook for 3 minutes, stirring or until warmed through.

When the pasta is cooked, drain and add it to the spinach sauce. Toss gently to combine.

To serve, top with toasted pine nuts.

REMIPE® FOR A GOOD NIGHT'S SLEEP

I used to try hard to stick with my 'protein and vegetables' for dinner, believing that eating carbohydrates for dinner would make me fat. No wonder I often had a disturbed night, since the amino acid tyrosine found in high-protein foods "wakes up" your brain.

Here is the good news: enjoying comforting pasta helps you sleep well by providing tryptophan from the pasta, egg and cheese. Your body converts tryptophan into hormones such as serotonin and melatonin, both of which have a relaxing and sleep-inducing effect.

Rest assured, you won't get fat by having a moderate serve of slow sugars such as pasta for dinner, as long as your breakfast and lunch are not full of them.

Oat porridge with maple syrup & cinnamon

serves 2

INGREDIENTS

120 g	rolled oats
200 ml	water
400 ml	milk (or a milk alternative such as soy, rice, or almond milk)
2	tablespoons maple syrup
½	teaspoon ground cinnamon

* For a variation, you can replace the maple syrup with a dollop of good orange marmalade.

METHOD

Place the oats, water and milk in a saucepan over high heat and bring to the boil.

Stir occasionally to prevent the mixture from catching on the bottom.

Turn the heat down to medium/low and cook for 10 minutes or until the oats are soft, remembering to stir occasionally.

Serve the oats porridge with ground cinnamon and maple syrup on top.

RE**M**IPE® FOR A GOOD NIGHT'S SLEEP

Just want to have a good night's sleep without spending too much time and energy cooking dinner?

Oat porridge is a delicious and easy way to induce restful slumber. It is a light dinner with low calories, yet it will make you feel content.

Oats, another complex carbohydrate, trigger a rise in blood sugar, which in turn triggers insulin production and the release of sleep-inducing brain chemicals.

Oats are rich in vitamin B6, an anti-stress vitamin, as well as melatonin.

Milk contains the amino acid L-tryptophan which turns to 5-HTP that has a positive effect on sleep and releases relaxing serotonin.

Chicken saltimbocca with spinach and nuts

INGREDIENTS

400 g	frozen spinach, thawed overnight
8	chicken thigh fillets, flattened (place chicken between two layers of baking paper and tap with a rolling pin)
8	slices prosciutto ham
1 ½	tablespoons Dijon mustard
30 g	Brazil nuts, finely chopped, plus 12 more to serve
½	cup white wine
30 g	walnuts, roughly chopped salt and pepper to season

serves 4

METHOD

Preheat oven to 180°C.

Place one piece of prosciutto on a clean, flat surface, then lay a piece of chicken on the prosciutto.

Brush chicken with ½ teaspoon Dijon mustard and add 1 tablespoon spinach in the middle. Sprinkle ½ teaspoon Brazil nuts on chicken and roll the chicken from one end to the other. Place the chicken roll on a wide baking dish, with the join on the bottom. Repeat the same process with the remaining chicken fillets.

Add white wine to the baking dish and bake for 20 minutes or until the chicken rolls are cooked.

Add remaining spinach to the baking dish. Spread the spinach between the chicken rolls and bake for a further 5 minutes.

Serve the chicken rolls with spinach and extra Brazil nuts. Sprinkle walnuts on top of the spinach.

REMIPE® FOR BEAUTIFUL HAIR

Nuts are generally good for your hair health. Brazil nuts are one of nature's best sources of selenium, an important mineral for the health of your scalp.

Walnuts contain alpha-linolenic acid, an Omega-3 fatty acid that may help condition your hair. They are also a terrific source of zinc, as are cashews, pecans, and almonds. A zinc deficiency can lead to hair shedding.

Chicken provides high quality protein that is critical in preventing weak, brittle hair and loss of hair colour.

It also provides iron with a high degree of bio-availability, meaning your body can easily reap its benefits.

Fried rice with carrot, ginger and coriander

serves 4

INGREDIENTS

2	tablespoons canola oil
20 g	butter
200 g	pork mince
1	cup grated carrot
1	onion, finely chopped
1	tablespoon grated ginger
3	cups cooked rice (refer to page 166 for brown rice remipe)
½	cup chicken stock
	salt and pepper to season
4	tablespoons chopped coriander

METHOD

Heat the oil and butter in a frying pan over medium heat.

Add pork and cook for 3 minutes while breaking lumps with a wooden spoon.

Add carrot, onion, ginger and cook for 5 minutes or until onion turns golden brown.

Add cooked brown rice and chicken stock and heat through.

Season with salt and pepper.

Sprinkle with coriander and serve.

RE**M**IPE®
FOR
BEAUTIFUL
HAIR

Carrots are very important for healthy hair and scalp as well as for our eyes and vision due to their high amount of vitamin A.

Pork mince is included to boost protein intake.

Without enough protein, your body can't replace the hair which you naturally shed every day resulting in dry, brittle and weak hair.

Salmon and Swiss chard pasta bake

serves 4

INGREDIENTS

200 g	ribbon pasta
2	tablespoons canola oil
20 g	butter
300 g	Swiss chard, roughly chopped
	Use the green part only, or substitute with spinach
	salt and pepper to season
300 g	salmon fillet
½	cup grated Parmesan or any other hard cheese such as Emmental, cheddar or mozzarella

METHOD

Preheat oven to 180°C.

Place the pasta in a large saucepan of lightly salted boiling water and cook for 7-8 minutes or until al dente. Set aside.

Heat the oil and butter in a frying pan over medium heat.

Add the Swiss chard and cook for 3 minutes or until it is bright green and wilted. Season with salt and pepper and set aside.

Cook salmon in the same frying pan for 2 minutes each side, taking care not to overcook the salmon.

Remove the skin from the salmon and flake it roughly with a fork.

Place pasta, Swiss chard and salmon in a baking dish.

Cover with grated cheese and bake in hot grill mode for 5 minutes or until golden brown.

REMIPE®
FOR
BEAUTIFUL
HAIR

Salmon is loaded with Omega-3 fatty acids. This high-quality protein source is also full of vitamin B12 and iron.

A deficiency in Omega-3 fatty acids can result in a dry scalp and hair, causing dull looking hair.

Spinach, broccoli and Swiss chard are excellent sources of vitamins A and C.

Your body needs vitamin A in order to produce sebum, an oily substance secreted by your hair follicles that is the body's natural hair conditioner.

Vitamin C stimulates hair growth.

Steamed oysters with soy sauce and spring onions

serves 2

INGREDIENTS

1 dozen fresh oysters in shells

Sauce
1 tablespoon soy sauce
½ tablespoon red wine vinegar
1 sprig spring onions, finely sliced

METHOD

Combine all sauce ingredients in a bowl.

Drop ¼ teaspoon of sauce onto each oyster shell.

Steam oysters for 3 minutes over boiling water.

Garnish with spring onions and serve immediately.

REMIPE® FOR BEAUTIFUL HAIR

Oysters are an impressive source of antioxidants which provide many hair health benefits.

If you feel wary of fresh oysters, this remipe provides you with the safety of cooked oysters and their beautiful taste.

Oysters are rich in zinc, a lack of which can lead to hair loss and a dry, flaky scalp.

Hair is made of about 97% protein.

Oysters can boast a good level of protein as well as zinc. Without enough protein, your body can't replace the hairs that you naturally shed every day, resulting in dry, brittle and weak hair.

Steamed salmon with fennel

serves 2

INGREDIENTS

1	tablespoon canola oil
15 g	butter
½	teaspoon salt
1	teaspoon sugar
3	baby fennel (or 1 big fennel) cut into wedges
½	cup white wine
2	salmon fillets
	salt and pepper to season
1	tablespoon lime juice

METHOD

Heat the oil, butter, salt and sugar in a saucepan over medium heat.

Add the fennel and cook for 3 minutes with the lid on. Turn the fennel over and cook for another 2 minutes, with the lid on, until all sides are golden brown.

Place the salmon on top of the fennel and pour the white wine over both.

Cover the saucepan with a lid and simmer for 3 minutes or until the salmon turns pink. Take care not to overcook the salmon.

Season with salt and pepper.

Sprinkle lime juice over the top and serve.

REMIPE®
FOR
BEAUTIFUL
HAIR

Salmon is the super food for your hair (and much else!).

This is the easiest remipe to help you eat delicious salmon with its many health benefits.

Keep this remipe in mind for days you simply don't have the time or energy to fuss with cooking.

BBQ mackerel with watercress, dill and walnut salad

serves 2

INGREDIENTS

250 g   mackerel fillets, cleaned
       canola oil spray or 1 teaspoon canola oil
       salt and pepper to season
1   bunch watercress, trimmed and washed
1   bunch dill leaves, finely chopped
50 g   dry roasted walnuts, roughly chopped

Salad dressing
1   teaspoon Dijon mustard
1   tablespoon white balsamic vinegar
1   teaspoon maple syrup
4   tablespoons extra virgin olive oil

METHOD

Heat your BBQ or grill to medium/high heat.

Spray or brush the mackerel with the oil and cook each side on the BBQ or grill for 3 to 5 minutes - or until cooked with brown marks.

Mackerel fillets will come off the BBQ easily once they're well cooked. If they stick to the BBQ, leave for another minute and try again. Season with salt and pepper.

While the mackerel is cooking, make your salad: place all ingredients for the dressing in a salad bowl and whisk well.

Add the watercress, dill and walnuts to the bowl. Combine with the salad dressing.

Serve mackerel fillets with salad.

REMIPE®
FOR
BEAUTIFUL
SKIN

You need to eat beautiful things to be beautiful.

This elegant and so-good-for-you remipe should be part of your repertoire as your edible beauty treatment.

To make eating your Omega 3-rich fish a regular and easy habit, you can buy frozen cleaned mackerel fillets from an Asian supermarket.

There's no need to thaw or do anything, just put the fish directly onto your BBQ.

You'll find flavour is not compromised by this convenience.

BBQ sardine and roasted red capsicum

INGREDIENTS

5   red capsicums, halved and de-seeded
2   cloves garlic, finely grated
2   tablespoons extra virgin olive oil
    salt and pepper to season
4   fresh or frozen sardines, cleaned

serves 4

METHOD

Preheat oven to 180°C.

Place capsicums skin side up on a lined baking tray. Bake for 35 minutes or until the skin is partly black.

Transfer capsicums from the oven to a bowl and cover with cling wrap. Set aside for 15 minutes.

Preheat BBQ or grill to medium/high heat.

Peel off the capsicum skin and arrange in a single layer on a wide plate. Sprinkle with garlic, salt and pepper and drizzle with olive oil.

Place sardines on the BBQ or grill and cook for 3-5 minutes per side (the cooking time will vary depending on whether you use fresh or frozen sardines) or cooked until golden brown.

Serve sardines and capsicum with whole grain bread.

REMIPE®
FOR
BEAUTIFUL
SKIN

Selenium is another trace mineral which is essential for good skin.

It's critical for making glutathione, an enzyme that helps to mop up the free radicals we inhale from air pollution and cigarette smoke.

If left to their own devices, these free radicals can rampage through the body and damage collagen and elastin in the skin.

Selenium-rich foods include Brazil nuts, lobster, tuna, lemon sole, squid, scallops, sardines, sunflower seeds, cashew nuts, mixed nuts, raisins and walnuts.

Red capsicum is full of vitamin C, an important antioxidant vitamin for healthy skin.

Scallops in curry coconut sauce with butternut pumpkin mash

serves 4

INGREDIENTS

1	butternut pumpkin, unpeeled and cut into big chunks for roasting (if you have a pumpkin of about 1 kilogram, you'll be able to divide it into 8 pieces)
2	tablespoons canola oil or oil spray to brush on the pumpkin
5	fresh sage leaves, finely chopped
12	scallops (pat dry with paper towel)
2	tablespoons canola oil
30 g	butter
	salt and pepper to season

Coconut curry sauce

50 g	coconut milk powder
1	teaspoon curry powder
1	teaspoon brown sugar
¼	teaspoon each of salt and pepper
100 ml	hot water

METHOD

Preheat oven to 180°C.

Brush or spray pumpkin with oil and place on a lined baking tray. Bake for 35 minutes and leave in the oven for 15 minutes after turning off the heat. This makes the pumpkin moist for mashing.

Take the pumpkin out of the oven and scrape the pumpkin from the skin. Place in a bowl and mash with a fork, just roughly. Add sage and mix. Keep the mash warm.

Combine all ingredients for the coconut curry sauce in a bowl and keep warm.

In a large frying pan, heat 1 tablespoon oil and 15 g butter over medium heat. Add half of the scallops, cooking for 1 minute on each side. Take care not to overcook, or the scallops will become rubbery. Repeat the process with oil, butter and the rest of the scallops.

Serve the scallops immediately with the sauce and pumpkin mash.

REMIPE®
FOR
BEAUTIFUL
SKIN

This remipe delivers an ample amount of selenium and vitamin A for your skin.

This dish is not only good for your skin, it's so simple and beautiful that you can cook it to entertain friends and family - you'll have the 'wow!' factor with its look and flavour.

If you cook the pumpkin mash in advance, the rest of this dish takes only 10 minutes to complete.

This remipe is ideal as a main course for your dinner party, as it can be put together quickly for serving.

Baked carrots with parmesan cheese and rosemary

INGREDIENTS

serves 4

2	tablespoons extra virgin olive oil
500 g	carrots, cut into chip size
¼	cup grated Parmesan cheese
2	teaspoons dried rosemary
	salt and pepper to season

METHOD

Preheat oven to 180°C.

Add carrots, Parmesan cheese, rosemary, salt and pepper in a plastic bag or bowl and mix well.

Spread carrots on a lined baking tray.

Bake for 20 minutes or until golden brown.

REMIPE® FOR BETTER EYESIGHT

Beta carotene is a substance that is converted to vitamin A in the human body. A half cup serving of cooked carrots contains four times the recommended daily intake of vitamin A.

Vitamin A plays an important role with eyesight in two ways: it helps in protecting the surface of the eyes (retina) and improves the vision in low light conditions.

In order to convert beta-carotene into vitamin A, the body also needs some fat, sufficient levels of zinc and iron along with good sanitary conditions, especially clean water. All must be available to avoid the carotene being flushed through the body with no effect.

This remipe goes well with meat, chicken or fish.

BBQ chicken kebab with honey and soy sauce

INGREDIENTS

serves 4

500 g	chicken thigh fillets, cut into bite-sized cubes

Marinade

2	tablespoons soy sauce
1	tablespoon rice vinegar
1	tablespoon honey
2	tablespoons canola oil
¼	teaspoon salt
¼	teaspoon pepper

METHOD

Soak bamboo skewers in water.

Place soy sauce, vinegar, honey, oil, salt and pepper in a plastic bag and mix well.

Add the chicken and marinate for a minimum 30 minutes (overnight is preferred).

Pierce 4-5 chicken pieces through soaked bamboo skewers.

Cook chicken on the grill or BBQ over medium to high heat.

Serve with cooked carrots to maximise beta-carotene conversion to vitamin A.

REMIPE® FOR BETTER EYESIGHT

This remipe accompanies the carrot remipe (page 48) in order to maximise beta-carotene conversion to vitamin A, by providing high levels of zinc and iron.

Chicken thighs and other dark meat cuts of chicken are great sources of zinc and iron. Chicken thighs have a lot more iron than chicken breasts, so it is a better poultry choice from a nutritional perspective, in addition to their great flavour.

In general, chicken also contains a form of iron (heme iron) that is most readily absorbed by your body.

Iron inhibitors in grains, legumes, nuts and seeds do not interfere with the absorption of iron in your chicken.

Steamed carrots with butter and dill

INGREDIENTS

300 g   carrots, washed
20 g   butter
½   tablespoon maple syrup
½   tablespoon lemon juice
2   tablespoons chopped fresh dill
    salt and pepper to season

METHOD

serves 2

Steam the carrots over boiling water for 15 minutes or until cooked to your taste.

Cut steamed carrots into 0.5 cm thick slices.

Place the carrots in a bowl and add the remaining ingredients.

Combine well and serve.

REMIPE® FOR BETTER EYESIGHT

Go carrots!

The abundant beta-carotene in carrots is also a powerful antioxidant that's effective in fighting against some forms of cancer.

Vitamin A converted from beta-carotene helps maintain the surface linings of the eyes and the respiratory, urinary, and intestinal tracts.

When those linings break down, bacteria can enter the body and cause infection. Vitamin A also helps maintain the integrity of skin and mucous membranes that function as a barrier to bacteria and viruses.

You can accompany this remipe with good sources of zinc and iron such as chicken, fish or meat to assist conversion from beta-carotene to vitamin A.

Pan-fried cuttle fish with lemon juice

INGREDIENTS

250 g	frozen or fresh cuttlefish fillets (if frozen, thaw and drain preferably overnight, otherwise pat dry with a paper towel)
2	tablespoons olive oil
½	tablespoon lemon juice
	salt and pepper to season

METHOD

serves 2

Score the outer skin of cuttlefish in a criss-cross pattern (run your knife 45° angle so you don't cut the fillet completely) and cut into squares of approximately 2 cm x 4 cm.

Heat a large frying pan over medium heat and add the oil and cuttlefish. Cook with the lid on for 3 minutes or until the cuttlefish turns light brown. Keep the lid on to prevent the oil from splattering.

Turn off the heat and add lemon juice.

Season with salt and pepper.

Serve with steamed carrots with butter and dill (page 52).

REMIPE® FOR BETTER EYESIGHT

Serve cuttlefish with the steamed carrots with butter and dill remipe (page 52) to maximise the benefits for your eyesight.

Cuttlefish has high levels of iron and zinc which effectively assist beta-carotene conversion to vitamin A. In addition, cuttlefish tastes fantastic.

I found cuttlefish is less tricky to cook than squid as it doesn't easily become rubbery when cooked.

Buy frozen cuttlefish if you want convenience. They are pre-cleaned and very delicious.

Creamed corn with fried eggs

INGREDIENTS

400 g	canned sweet corn, rinsed and drained (alternatively, 2 fresh ears of corn, husked)
30 g	butter
½	cup water
½	cup milk
	salt and pepper to season
1	tablespoon canola oil
4	eggs
2	tablespoons chopped chives to garnish

serves 2

METHOD

If using fresh corn, cut the tip off the cob and cut the kernels from the cob with a small paring knife. Using the back of the blade, scrape against the cob to press out the milky liquid.

Place the corn kernels, butter, water and milk in a medium sauce pan. Bring to the boil and cook over medium/low heat with a lid on for 5 minutes or until soft.

Using a Bamix or food processor, roughly blend the cooked corn kernels. Season with salt and pepper.

Add the oil to a medium frying pan over medium heat and cook the eggs to your liking.

Garnish with chives and serve.

REMIPE® FOR BLADDER AND URINARY TRACT INFECTIONS

A simple and effective treatment for a person who is prone to urinary tract infections is to increase their fluid consumption in order to flush the urinary system.

Drinking cranberry or blueberry juice is encouraged as these juices contain proanthocyanidins which prevent bacteria from sticking to the lining of the bladder.

Corn acidifies the urine and helps decrease the bacterial growth.

Puy lentil with walnut & cranberry

serves 4

INGREDIENTS

300 g	lentils, rinsed and drained
1.2	litres of water
100 g	walnuts, chopped and dry roasted
80 g	dried cranberries
1	tablespoon cumin seed, dry roasted
4	tablespoons chopped parsley

Dressing

1 ½	tablespoons lemon juice
5	tablespoons extra virgin olive oil
1	teaspoon ground cumin
¼	teaspoon each of salt and pepper

METHOD

Place lentils and water in a medium saucepan and bring to the boil.

Simmer for 20 minutes over medium heat, or until lentils are cooked to your liking. Drain and set aside.

Place all dressing ingredients in a salad bowl and whisk well.

Add lentils, walnuts, cranberries and cumin seeds to the salad bowl.

Serve the lentil salad sprinkled with parsley on top.

REMIPE® FOR BLADDER AND URINARY TRACT INFECTIONS

This remipe can speed up healing of urinary tract infections (UTIs) and help prevent their recurrence.

Nutritional interventions for UTIs include eating foods that increase acidity levels in urine to help decrease bacterial growth.

Foods that increase acidity levels in urine are cranberries, corn, plums, prunes, lentils, bread products, peanuts and walnuts.

Stir-fried chicken with yellow capsicum, thyme and parsley

serves 4

INGREDIENTS

2	tablespoons canola oil
15 g	butter
400 g	chicken thigh fillets, cut into bite-sized pieces
2	yellow capsicum, cut into thin strips
½	teaspoon salt
15	sprigs of fresh thyme leaves (or 1 teaspoon dried thyme)
100 ml	white wine
4	tablespoons chopped parsley
	salt and pepper to season

METHOD

Heat the oil and butter in a frying pan over medium heat. Add the chicken and cook for 5 minutes or until golden brown. Set aside and keep warm.

Add the capsicum and salt to the same pan and stir-fry for 2 minutes over high heat.

Add the chicken, thyme and wine and cook for another 2 minutes or until the wine boils. Season with salt and pepper.

Sprinkle with parsley and serve with crusty bread.

REMIPE®
FOR
BLEEDING
GUMS

Bleeding gums are often associated with scurvy, a disease caused by a deficiency in vitamin C.

This remipe is packed with high vitamin C food sources.

Yellow capsicum provides 184 mg of vitamin C per 100 g serving, which is 206% of the recommended daily intake.

Fresh and dried herbs are packed with vitamins and health benefits. Thyme and parsley top the rank of herbs with high levels of vitamin C.

Kiwi and papaya salad

INGREDIENTS

2	kiwi fruit, peeled and cut into a half-moon shape
150 g	papaya, seeds scraped, cut into bite-sized pieces
1	teaspoon maple syrup
½	tablespoon freshly squeezed lime juice

serves 2

METHOD

Combine kiwi fruit, papaya and maple syrup in a bowl.

Sprinkle with lime juice and serve.

REMIPE® FOR BLEEDING GUMS

This is a delicious vitamin C-packed dessert recipe.

Vitamin A, D and E are also considered as critical nutrients for healthy gums as well as vitamin C.

Food sources for these vitamins include the following:

• Vitamin A: milk, cheese, fish, meat, breads, cereals, fruit, and vegetables
• Vitamin C: fruit, vegetables, chicken and beef
• Vitamin D: milk, cheese and tuna
• Vitamin E: vegetable oils, nuts and leafy vegetables

Puy lentil salad with eggs

INGREDIENTS

200 g	puy lentils, rinsed and drained (you can use tinned lentils to save time)
600 - 800 ml	water (about three times the volume of the lentils)
50 g	walnuts, chopped
½	tablespoon canola oil
2	eggs

Dressing

1	tablespoon raspberry vinegar
1	teaspoon maple syrup
3	tablespoons extra virgin olive oil
	salt and pepper to season

METHOD

serves 2

Place lentils and water in a medium saucepan and bring to the boil. Reduce heat to medium/low and simmer with the lid on for 20 minutes or until soft. Drain water and set aside.

In a frying pan, pan-fry the walnuts over low heat without oil until they are aromatic and golden. Set aside.

Mix all the dressing ingredients in a jar and shake well with the lid tightly on.

Combine cooked lentils, walnuts and dressing in a large bowl. Add the oil in the frying pan and cook eggs (sunny side up).

Serve with the lentil salad.

* Fresh lentils do not require soaking prior to cooking, however pre-soaking will reduce the cooking time by roughly half.

REMIPE® FOR BRITTLE NAILS

If you have brittle nails, consider eating foods that contain biotin, a B vitamin. Biotin can help your nails grow thicker and become stronger.

Foods containing high levels of biotin include peanuts, lentils, egg yolks, sardines, mushrooms, bananas, liver and cauliflower.

Zinc also helps with brittle nails. Foods rich in zinc include meat, shellfish and eggs.

Sautéed chicken liver with braised spinach

INGREDIENTS

Part 1

1	tablespoon canola oil
15 g	butter
250 g	spinach, cleaned and drained
2	cloves garlic, chopped
½	tablespoon lemon juice
¼	teaspoon nutmeg, ground
	salt and pepper to season

Part 2

1	tablespoon canola oil
15 g	butter
200 g	chicken liver
½	tablespoon Dijon mustard
2	tablespoons white wine (or Cognac if available)
2	tablespoons chopped parsley

METHOD

serves 2

Part 1
Heal the oil and butter in a frying pan over medium heat.

Add spinach and garlic and cook for 2 minutes or until wilted.

Sprinkle with lemon juice and nutmeg. Season with salt and pepper. Set aside and keep warm.

Part 2
In the same frying pan, heat the oil and butter over medium heat.

Add the chicken liver and mustard and cook for 3 minutes.

Turn the liver over to the other side. Add white wine (or Cognac) and cook for another 3 minutes or until the chicken liver is cooked well.

Place the chicken liver on the bed of spinach. Garnish with parsley and serve.

* Crusty bread goes well with this dish.

REMIPE®
FOR
BRITTLE
NAILS

Chicken liver has exceptionally high levels of biotin.

Use organic if you can - I highly recommend it, especially for meat that is organs of an animal such as liver and kidney.

Iron is another important nutrient in treating brittle nails and no other vegetable beats spinach in iron levels.

Chicken soup with ginger

INGREDIENTS

serves 5

1	whole organic chicken, rinsed (or use two spatchcocks if you prefer)
	Enough water to cover the chicken
5	cloves garlic
5 cm	piece ginger, sliced
2	carrots
1	medium sized onion
3	whole peppercorns (any colour)
2	stalks of celery
	Baby spinach (pre-washed is handy)

Sauce for the chicken

2	tablespoons sesame oil
1	teaspoon of salt
½	teaspoon pepper

METHOD

Place the chicken in a big pot. Add enough water to cover the chicken. Add all remaining ingredients except spinach and the sauce.

Bring to the boil over high heat, removing the foamy substance until there is a minimal amount left.

Reduce heat to medium/low and simmer for about an hour with the lid on.

Take the chicken out of the pot and keep warm. Discard vegetables (these have given out all their goodness to the soup) and bring the remaining liquid to the boil.

Turn off the heat and add spinach.

Serve chicken with the sauce (sesame oil, salt and pepper mixture) and a bowl of chicken soup.

REMIPE® FOR COLD AND FLU

Known as Jewish Penicillin, chicken soup has a long-held tradition of curing the common cold and flu.

Chicken soup actually has a mild medicinal effect, inhibiting inflammation of the cells in the nasal passage, therefore, reducing the symptoms of a cold.

For this remipe, you don't have to be rigid when measuring ingredients, just remember to add a little of this and a little of that. Have a bowl of soup several times a day.

A hot, thin soup will make you feel instantly better by relieving your congestion.

You can skim the fat off the next morning for a cleaner taste and lower calories.

Apple and rice porridge with a touch of ginger & honey

serves 2

INGREDIENTS

100 g	apple, peeled and diced
½	cup of long grain rice (any rice will suit, but Basmati or Jasmine cooks quickly)
3	cups water
1	teaspoon grated ginger
1	tablespoon honey

METHOD

Place apple, rice, water and ginger in a saucepan and bring to the boil.

Reduce heat to low and simmer for fifteen minutes.

Serve the porridge with a drizzle of honey.

REMIPE® FOR COLD AND FLU

Cold and flu often reduce our sense of taste and smell, resulting in loss of appetite and desire to cook.

If you're on your own when you're sick and don't have the energy to put together a chicken soup, then this remipe is for you.

This simple and nourishing remipe will provide you with vitamin C from the apple, plus zinc and energy from the rice. Ginger will act as an antacid to combat nausea. Honey is naturally antibacterial.

Poached salmon with lemon and dill

INGREDIENTS

500 g	salmon fillet
500 g	potatoes, cut into bite sizes (keep the skin on if organic)
20 g	butter
1	tablespoon lemon juice
200 g	quark cheese (German cream cheese)
2	tablespoons chopped dill

METHOD

serves 4

Steam the potatoes over boiling water for 15 minutes or until potatoes are cooked.

Poach salmon fillets in the boiling water you used for steaming the potatoes for 3 minutes or until the salmon is cooked. Take care not to overcook the salmon.

Serve potatoes and salmon on a plate, topped with butter, lemon juice, quark cheese and dill.

* Substitute quark cheese with ricotta cheese or thick Greek yoghurt if unavailable.

REMIPE® FOR COLD SORES

You can manage the outbreak of a cold sore by keeping your lysine level high.

The main cause of cold sores is the oral herpes virus in your body. Arginine, a simple common amino acid that is quite similar to lysine, is the main building material used by the cells to create a new herpes virus.

Cells store lysine in the same area as arginine. If the cell has more lysine in storage, it then has much less room for arginine.

This remipe consists of food high in lysine levels, therefore will help reduce the length and severity of a cold sore outbreak.

Vanilla ice cream with mango

INGREDIENTS

150 ml vanilla ice cream
1   mango, cut into small pieces

serves 1

METHOD

Serve ice cream topped with mango.

* Do not use chocolate ice cream or ice cream containing nuts for this remipe. Chocolate and most types of nuts contain a high amount of arginine which promotes the virus that causes herpes. Avoid foods that are high in arginine such as orange juice, Tahini paste, sesame seeds, pumpkin seeds, blackberries and blueberries.

REMIPE® FOR COLD SORES

You should not feel guilty about indulging in ice cream since it helps alleviate cold sores.

Sounds too good to be true?

Dairy products, including cheese, yoghurt and ice cream, are high in lysine that helps stop the virus that causes herpes. Mangos, avocados, apples, pears, tomatoes, apricots, figs, beets and papaya are also high in lysine.

Vanilla ice cream with fresh mango is a decadent way to recover from your cold sore.

Substitute ice cream with yoghurt (also high in lysine) if you're watching your waistline.

Yoghurt with banana, honey and almond

INGREDIENTS

serves 1

METHOD

150 g   plain yoghurt
1   banana, mashed with a fork (tastes sweeter this way without adding sugar!)
1   tablespoon honey
A handful of almond flakes

* Full fat yogurt is recommended since the low fat ones are less tasty and tend to contain more sugar than the full fat ones to compensate for the lack of taste.

Place all ingredients on top of each other in the order listed and serve.

REMIPE®
FOR
COMBATING
STRESS

Are you so stressed out that the last thing you want to worry about is what to cook? If so, then this remipe is the answer. You'll hardly have to cook a thing, yet it will make you feel much less stressed after eating this dish.

Banana is known for its high potassium level, one of the nutrients depleted by the high metabolic rate caused by stress.

Almond and honey are high in B vitamins and magnesium both involved in the production of serotonin, helping regulate moods and relieving stress.

Dairy products including yoghurt are also a great source of the vitamin B group, including B1, B2, B5, B6 and B12.

Fried rice with spinach and tofu

INGREDIENTS

2	tablespoons canola oil
200 g	spinach, washed and roughly chopped (or use pre-washed baby spinach to save time)
300 g	cooked brown rice (see page 166 for how to cook brown rice)
250 g	tofu (medium hard type) mashed with a fork
1	tablespoon roasted sesame seed oil

Sauce

3	tablespoons Xiao Xing wine
2	tablespoons Soy Sauce
1	tablespoon rice vinegar
½	teaspoon salt
1	teaspoon sugar

METHOD

serves 2

Heat 1 tablespoon oil in a wok over high heat. Add spinach and stir-fry until spinach is wilted and bright green. Set aside.

Heat 1 tablespoon oil in the wok over high heat. Add cooked rice and stir-fry for 2 minutes.

Combine all sauce ingredients in a small bowl.

Add the tofu and sauce mixture to the wok and cook for 3 minutes or until the liquid is almost absorbed by the rice.

Add spinach and sesame seed oil and cook for one minute or until combined and heated through.

REMIPE® FOR COMBATING STRESS

This is a healthy and comforting Asian remipe to help you relieve stress.

Vitamin B and magnesium are required for the production of serotonin which helps regulate mood and lower stress.

Brown rice and green leafy vegetables are rich sources of B vitamins. Tofu is also a rich source of magnesium.

Hummus dip with vegetable sticks

serves 4

INGREDIENTS

Hummus
1   can of chickpeas, rinsed and drained
2   tablespoons extra virgin olive oil, plus
    some more to serve
1   tablespoon tahini (ground sesame paste)
2   tablespoons lemon juice
2   tablespoons water
2   cloves garlic
    salt and pepper to season

Vegetable sticks
2   stalks of celery, cut into thin sticks
2   carrots, cut into thin sticks

METHOD

Process all hummus ingredients in a food processor.

Drizzle olive oil over the top and serve with vegetable sticks.

Season with salt and pepper.

REMIPE® FOR CONSTIPATION

The most important aspect of eating to ease constipation is to slowly increase your intake of dietary fibre. Drinking a lot of water is the next important thing in order to relieve constipation.

Focus on eating a wide variety of fruits, vegetables, nuts, legumes and whole grains, as they contain plenty of dietary fibre.

Many products are advertised as being 'multi-grain', but are actually poor sources of whole grains.

The only way to know for sure is to carefully read the list of ingredients. In order to be a good source of fibre, the very first word should be 'whole'.

Seaweed salad with grapefruit

serves 2

INGREDIENTS

Salad

20 g	dried seaweed (wakame)
100 g	cherry tomatoes, halved
100 g	baby bocconcini cheese, rinsed and drained
1	pink or yellow grapefruit, peeled by segment

Dressing

½	teaspoon wasabi (Japanese green mustard)
2	tablespoons soy sauce
1	tablespoon rice vinegar
2	tablespoons olive oil
1	tablespoon sesame seed oil
½	teaspoon maple syrup
	salt and pepper to season

METHOD

Soak seaweed in plenty of water for 10 minutes and drain well.

Place all dressing ingredients in a jar and shake well, with the lid tightly on.

Squeeze excess water from seaweed with two hands and cut to roughly 3 cm lengths, using scissors.

Gently combine all salad ingredients with the sauce to serve.

REMIPE® FOR CONSTIPATION

If you are prone to constipation, relief via a laxative is drastic and doesn't last for long.

New habits need to be established as a long term resolution such as drinking lots of water, eating more fresh and cooked vegetables to increase fibre intake.

Seaweed is nature's wonder food for smooth bowel movements, resulting in good intestinal health and radiant skin.

This salad is refreshing, delicious and will energise you to your maximum potential.

Beef and radish consommé

INGREDIENTS

800 g	radish or daikon, cut into square shapes (approximately 2 x 2 cm square and 3 mm thick)
200 g	beef (scotch fillet or rump steak) cut into small cubes
1	onion, peeled and halved
1	tablespoon grated ginger
500 ml	beef stock
300 ml	water
	salt and pepper to season
2	tablespoons chopped spring onions

serves 4

METHOD

Place all ingredients in a saucepan except the salt and pepper.

Bring to boil over medium heat, and then reduce heat to low and simmer for 15 minutes.

Season with salt and pepper.

Garnish with spring onions and serve.

REMIPE® FOR COUGHS

Common causes of coughs include irritation or inflammation of the throat, post-nasal drip or regurgitation of stomach acid from heartburn.

Warm fluid thins mucus, therefore clear soup and warm honey water are good remipes when you have a cough. Also, make sure your room is moist enough so your throat doesn't get dry.

The chicken soup remipe for the common cold on page 68 will also help alleviate a cough. Radish is rich in vitamin C which is an important vitamin in the fight against a cold or a cough.

Use the green leaves of the radish for salad if available; radish greens contain 6 times more vitamin C than the root.

Orange, strawberry and grape salad

INGREDIENTS

serves 4

METHOD

1 orange, peeled and segmented
1 punnet of strawberries (about 250 g), cleaned and halved
1 bunch of green grapes (purple grapes are fine, but green makes a prettier colour combination)
1 tablespoon freshly squeezed lemon juice
1 tablespoon honey (Use Manuka honey if available since it has anti-bacterial and anti-viral properties)

Combine oranges, strawberries and grapes in a salad bowl.

Sprinkle with lemon juice and drizzle honey over the salad.

Serve immediately.

REMIPE®
FOR
COUGHS

This one brings a punch of vitamin C to combat a cough. These three fruits are high in vitamin C and also make a great taste combination.

The mix of red, orange and green is beautiful to look at, and that'll help cheer you up in this tough time! Eat a moderate portion, though, since fruit contains sugar which feeds and multiplies bacteria.

If your sleep is easily disturbed, have this salad in the morning or early afternoon rather than in the evening. High levels of vitamin C may hinder a good night's sleep.

French mussel soup

INGREDIENTS

serves 4

2 kg	mussels (use pre-cleaned mussels to save time)
1	tablespoon canola oil
15 g	butter
200 g	onion, chopped
1	stalk of celery, chopped
4	garlic cloves, chopped
8	sprigs thyme (or 2 teaspoons dried thyme)
2	bay leaves
400 ml	dry white wine
150 ml	water
200 ml	single cream
4	tablespoons parsley, chopped
	cooked brown rice (see page 166 for cooking instruction) or crusty bread
	pepper to season

METHOD

Clean and rinse mussels if you haven't bought the pre-cleaned ones. Drain and set aside.

Add the oil and butter to a medium saucepan over medium heat.

Add the onion and celery and cook for 4 minutes or until they are soft.

Add garlic, thyme, bay leaves, wine and water and bring to the boil.

Add the mussels, cover the pan tightly and simmer over low heat for 2-3 minutes, shaking occasionally.

Turn off the heat and discard unopened mussels.

Add the cream and season with pepper.

Sprinkle with the parsley and serve with cooked brown rice or bread.

REMIPE® FOR CRACKS AT THE CORNERS OF YOUR MOUTH

This condition is called angular cheilitis, also known as angular stomatitis.

The main cause of this condition is frequent or persistent saliva touching the skin outside the mouth, so do not lick your lips.

The cracks and the excess moisture provide a fertile environment for yeast which causes infection, and this leads to further irritation.

In addition to taking medicine according to your doctor's advice, it is good to add vitamin B12 (Cobalamin) to your diet, since vitamin B12 helps tremendously in fighting bacteria and fungus.

* B12-rich foods include shellfish (mussels, clams, oysters), liver (lamb and beef are the highest sources), caviar (fish eggs), octopus, fish (mackerel and salmon are the highest), crab, lobster, beef, lamb, cheese and eggs.

Spaghetti Alle Vongole

INGREDIENTS

400 g	thin spaghetti
1 kg	small clams (scrubbed and cleaned)
1	bunch parsley leaves, chopped
½	teaspoon chilli flakes (or one tablespoon chopped fresh red chilli without the seeds)
3	garlic cloves, finely chopped
½	cup dry white wine
½	cup olive oil
	salt and pepper to season

METHOD

serves 4

Cook the spaghetti in a large saucepan filled with salted boiling water for 8-10 minutes or until al dente.

While the pasta is cooking, combine all the remaining ingredients in a saucepan except salt and pepper.

Bring to the boil with the pan tightly covered. Simmer over low heat for 2-3 minutes, shaking the pan occasionally.

Turn off the heat and discard any unopened clams.

Drain the pasta and add to the clam sauce. Combine the pasta and sauce over low heat until warmed through.

Season with salt and pepper and serve.

REMIPE® FOR CRACKS AT THE CORNERS OF YOUR MOUTH

Clams are another rich source of vitamin B12 that helps in fighting fungal infection at the corners of your mouth.

Sometimes angular cheilitis is caused by an iron deficiency. Parsley contains high amounts of iron. With this remipe, you get to eat lots of parsley effortlessly.

This dish is simple to cook, yet sophisticated enough to star as the main dish at a dinner party. It's a delicious way to cure yourself.

Rice porridge

INGREDIENTS

½ cup Basmati or Jasmine rice, rinsed
and drained
3 cups water

METHOD

serves 2

Place rice and water in a medium saucepan and bring to the boil.

Simmer for 15 minutes or until rice is soft and the porridge thickens slightly.

Serve the porridge in small amounts, several times if necessary.

* You can use any type of white rice for this remipe. Adjust the cooking time since some types of rice take longer to make porridge.

REMIPE® FOR DIARRHOEA

A mild episode of diarrhoea will clear up on its own in a few days.

Diarrhoea is normally caused by bacteria or viruses found in infected foods or transmitted from one person to another.

Drink plenty of water and clear liquids such as thin soups and weak tea to prevent dehydration.

This remipe will ease the symptoms of diarrhoea and help prevent dehydration.

Pumpkin soup

INGREDIENTS

300 g	Jap or butternut pumpkin, peeled and cut into small pieces
½	cup Basmati or Jasmine rice, rinsed and drained
4	cups water
	salt to season

serves 4

METHOD

Place pumpkin, rice and water in a medium saucepan and bring to the boil.

Simmer for 20 minutes or until the pumpkin and rice are soft.

Blend the soup with a Bamix or in a food processor until it becomes thin enough to drink from a cup. Add boiled water if necessary.

Season with salt.

Have a small bowl of soup several times a day.

REMIPE® FOR DIARRHOEA

This thin pumpkin soup remipe is easy on your stomach and delivers some level of fibre to ease diarrhoea.

You can eat this when you feel bored with rice porridge, which is also a sign that your body is recovering from the diarrhoea.

Tuna steak with wasabi yoghurt dressing and avocado salad

serves 4

INGREDIENTS

Yoghurt dressing
100 ml   yoghurt + ½ teaspoon wasabi paste + 1 teaspoon probiotic powder (if available) + salt and pepper to season

Avocado salad
1 ½   tablespoons lemon juice
3   tablespoons extra virgin olive oil
2   avocados, cut into cubes
2   ripe tomatoes, cut into cubes
2   stems spring onions, sliced thinly
     salt and pepper to season

Tuna steak
1   tablespoon canola oil to brush on the tuna
600 g   tuna, cut into steak shapes

METHOD

Combine all ingredients for the yoghurt dressing in a bowl and set aside.

Combine all ingredients for the avocado salad in a bowl and set aside.

Heat a grill or BBQ over high heat. Brush tuna steaks with oil and cook for 1 minute per side.

Double-wrap the tuna in cooking foil and set aside for 5 minutes.

Serve the tuna with yoghurt dressing and avocado salad.

REMIPE® FOR ECZEMA

Malnutrition is one of the contributing factors of eczema. Individuals with eczema usually have deficiencies in Omega-3 and Omega-6 essential fatty acids (EFAs).

This remipe is made from foods high in Omega-3 essential fatty acids.

Good sources of Omega-3 EFAs are: Atlantic salmon, herrings, sardines, tuna, mackerel and wild game such as venison and buffalo.

You will get sufficient levels of Omega 6 EFAs by using sunflower, corn or safflower oil in your cooking.

Yoghurt is another food that is known to be beneficial in treating eczema. The probiotics in yoghurt benefit the immune system, especially many of the immune cells located in the intestinal tract.

Chickpea curry with yoghurt and brown rice

serves 4

INGREDIENTS

1	tablespoon canola oil
1	teaspoon grated ginger
2	cloves garlic, chopped
2	bay leaves
1	large onion, chopped
1	teaspoon each cinnamon powder, turmeric powder, ground coriander and ground cumin
2	teaspoons brown sugar
1	can chickpeas, rinsed and drained
150 ml	chicken stock or water
1	can tomatoes (chopped or whole) salt and pepper to season
4	tablespoons chopped fresh coriander
300 g	cooked brown rice (see page 166 for cooking instruction), plus 200 ml yoghurt to serve

METHOD

Heat the oil in a medium saucepan over medium heat. Add ginger, garlic, bay leaves and onion and cook for 2 minutes or until the onion is soft.

Add cinnamon, turmeric, clove, coriander, cumin and sugar and cook for another minute.

Add chickpeas, stock (or water) and tomatoes (break the tomatoes with a wooden spoon if whole) and simmer for 10 minutes over low heat with the pan covered.

Season with salt and pepper.

Serve the curry with yoghurt and brown rice sprinkled with fresh coriander.

REMIPE®
FOR
ECZEMA

Vegetarian diets improve the symptoms of atopic dermatitis. This includes beans, lentils, pulses, soy products, nuts and seeds.

Natural bio-yoghurt can help to replenish good gut bacteria.

This is a very simple curry dish using pantry dried spices without the hassle of making a paste.

Roasted carrot and pumpkin soup

INGREDIENTS

3	tablespoons canola oil
300 g	carrots, cut into small chunks for roasting
600 g	pumpkin (jack or butternut pumpkin is preferred), cut to similar size as the carrots
2	medium sized onions, chopped
4	cloves garlic
1	teaspoon ground nutmeg
500 ml	water
700 ml	chicken stock
	salt and pepper to season

METHOD

serves 4

Preheat oven to 180°C.

Mix 2 tablespoons oil with carrots and pumpkin and bake for 30 minutes. Leave cooked pumpkin in the oven for 15 minutes after turning the heat off.

Heat 1 tablespoon oil in a medium saucepan and cook the onion for 3 minutes or until soft over medium heat. Add garlic and nutmeg and cook for another 2 minutes.

Add roasted carrot, pumpkin, water and stock to the onion mixture.

Bring to the boil over high heat. Reduce heat to low and simmer for 10 minutes.

Blend the soup (using a stick blender is handy) and season with salt and pepper.

Serve with slices of toasted whole grain bread.

In order for you to build a stronger immune system, it's crucial to consume the recommended 3-5 servings of carotenoid-rich fruits and vegetables daily.

The rule of thumb is to look for yellow and orange coloured produce, as these are great sources of carotenoid-rich fruits and vegetables: oranges, pumpkins, carrots, sweet potatoes etc.

Roasted sweet potato and Danish feta salad

serves 2

INGREDIENTS

500 g	sweet potatoes, peeled and cut into small pieces
2	tablespoons canola oil (or use spray oil for convenience)
½	teaspoon salt
½	teaspoon pepper
100 g	Danish feta cheese
2	tablespoons chopped spring onions
2	tablespoons dry roasted pine nuts
1	tablespoon freshly squeezed lemon juice
2	tablespoons extra virgin olive oil

METHOD

Preheat oven to 180°C.

Mix the oil, salt and pepper with sweet potatoes and bake for 30 minutes. Leave cooked sweet potatoes in the oven for 15 minutes after turning the heat off.

Place sweet potatoes on a serving plate and crumble feta cheese over the top.

Sprinkle with spring onions and pine nuts.

Combine lemon juice with the olive oil and drizzle the mixture over the sweet potato salad.

REMIPE® FOR ENHANCING IMMUNITY

Being mindful of the need to increase your intake of yellow and orange coloured vegetables to strengthen your immunity, sweet potato is another excellent and delicious choice.

For this remipe use Danish feta rather than the alternatives, since Danish feta is less salty and has a distinctive flavour that is well matched to the sweet potatoes.

Enjoy this delicious immunity booster.

Rocket and macadamia nut salad

serves 2

INGREDIENTS

100 g   rocket leaves (use pre-washed ones
         to save time)
         A handful of macadamia nuts (raw and
         unsalted), finely chopped or processed

         Salad dressing
   1   teaspoon curry powder
   1   teaspoon maple syrup
   1   teaspoon white balsamic vinegar
   2   tablespoons extra virgin olive oil
   ½   teaspoon salt
   ½   teaspoon pepper

METHOD

Wash and dry the rocket leaves.

Mix all dressing ingredients together in a jar and
shake well, with the lid tightly on.

Dress rocket leaves with the salad dressing just
prior to serving.

REMIPE® FOR ENHANCING IMMUNITY

This salad goes very well with soup remipes for enhancing immunity, adding more vitamin E to your meal.

Vitamin E protects your body from free radicals which cause cardio disease and cancer. The olive oil, macadamia nuts and rocket in this remipe are full of vitamin E.

This salad is aromatic and goes well with eggs, chicken or beef dishes.

Stir-fried chicken, broccoli and red capsicum

serves 4

INGREDIENTS

3	tablespoons canola oil (grapeseed or peanut oil is also good, since they have a high smoking point)
500 g	chicken thigh fillets, cut into bite-sized pieces
500 g	broccoli, cut into florets
1	red capsicum, thinly sliced into long strips
100 g	(or ½ cup) unsalted roasted cashews
4	cups cooked brown rice (See page 166 for cooking instructions)

Sauce

3	tablespoons Xiao Xing wine
2	tablespoons soy sauce
1	teaspoon salt
2	teaspoons sugar
1	tablespoon rice vinegar
2	teaspoons cornflour

METHOD

Heat 1 tablespoon of oil in a wok over high heat. Add half the chicken and stir-fry for 2 minutes or until golden. Repeat with the remaining chicken and set aside.

Heat 1 tablespoon of oil in the wok over high heat. Add capsicum and stir-fry for 2 minutes. Set aside.

Heat 1 tablespoon of oil in the wok over high heat. Add broccoli and stir-fry for 2 minutes or until bright green and tender-crisp.

Combine sauce ingredients in a small bowl.

Add chicken, sauce mixture, capsicum and cashews. Stir-fry until combined and heated through.

Serve with rice.

REMIPE®
FOR ENHANCING IMMUNITY

This remipe is full of vitamin C (broccoli and red capsicum) and zinc (chicken). Vitamin C and zinc are considered as important nutrients to build a strong immune system.

Both vitamin C and zinc are easily lost via prolonged heat, so a quick stir-fry is a perfect method to retain these nutrients as much as possible.

Not only good nutritionally, these three ingredients make a great colour and taste combination. Enjoy with a bowl of rice.

Bircher Muesli with Goji berries

INGREDIENTS

Part 1

250 g	rolled oats
700 ml	milk or milk substitute
250 ml	yoghurt
100 g	sultanas

Part 2

1	big apple (or 2 small apples), shredded
½	cup almond flakes, toasted
½	cup Goji berries
2	tablespoons maple syrup

serves 4

METHOD

Mix all 'Part 1' ingredients and rest for a minimum of 2 hours, or preferably overnight in the fridge, before you eat.

Refrigerate until you eat - up to 2 days, if the milk is fresh.

To serve, add 'Part 2' ingredients on top of the 'Part 1' mixture.

* Use a Japanese mandoline to julienne apples quickly and with ease.

REM**IPE**®
FOR
FATIGUE

Oats contain high levels of magnesium, protein and phosphorous. These three nutrients significantly affect energy levels, making oats an ideal food for combating fatigue.

Also, oats are a good source of vitamin B1 (thiamine) which is crucial for producing energy.

This remipe doesn't involve cooking but requires resting for a couple of hours, or preferably overnight, before you eat.

It is good as a breakfast but I sometimes eat it as a dinner when I am too tired to cook. It helps me sleep well too.

Three bean soup with Rosemary

serves 4

INGREDIENTS

2   tablespoons canola oil
1   tablespoon butter or coconut oil
3   cloves garlic, chopped
2   tablespoons fresh rosemary or
     1 tablespoon dry rosemary leaves
3   anchovy fillets
1   onion, finely chopped
2   stalks of celery, finely chopped
2   carrots, finely chopped
3   cans of different beans - cannellini,
     borlotti and butter beans, for example
1   can chopped tomatoes
400 ml   water
500 ml   chicken stock
     salt and pepper to season

METHOD

Heat the oil and butter in a large saucepan over low to medium heat.

Add garlic, rosemary, anchovies and cook for 2 minutes. Break up the anchovies with a wooden spoon while cooking.

Add onion, celery and carrots and cook for a further 5 minutes over medium heat or until vegetables are soft.

Rinse and drain the beans. Add the beans, tomatoes, water and stock to the pan and bring to the boil. Simmer for 15 minutes over medium to low heat.

Season with salt and pepper.

REMIPE® FOR FATIGUE

Beans are known as a miracle food for their nutritional value.

Beans are a concentrated source of stable and slow burning energy due to their unique nutritional composition.

All types of beans are low in fat, high in fibre, and provide a good balance of carbohydrates and protein.

The protein and high fibre content in beans work together to help balance blood sugar and prevent spikes and dips in energy.

You cannot resist eating them when you know how good they are. They are very delicious too!

Banana and peanut butter sandwich with chocolate milk

serves 1

INGREDIENTS

1	banana, sliced
1	tablespoon peanut butter
½	tablespoon honey
2	slices sandwich bread
250 ml	chocolate milk

METHOD

Spread peanut butter on a slice of bread.

Top with banana and drizzle with honey.

Cover with the other slice of bread.

Serve with a glass of chocolate milk.

REMIPE®
FOR
HANGOVER

This is a folklore remipe for hangover.

Banana is rich in vitamin B6 which is one of the vitamins most depleted by alcohol. Banana is also rich in antacid, combating nausea. It's full of potassium and magnesium which relax pounding blood vessels that lead to headaches...nearly a super food!

Chocolate milk also acts as a soothing coat for your stomach, relieving nausea. Many have testified to this remipe!

Skip the peanut butter if your stomach feels weak.

The 2am pig-out pasta

INGREDIENTS

serves 2

200 g   thin spaghetti pasta
100 g   bacon, chopped into small pieces
100 g   single cream
2   eggs
2   tablespoons Parmesan cheese, in
    powder form or freshly grated

METHOD

Cook the pasta in a large saucepan of salted boiling water for 7-8 minutes or until al dente.

While the pasta is cooking, place the bacon in a medium frying pan over medium heat and cook for 3-4 minutes or until crispy.

Add the pasta, cream, eggs and stir through over low heat.

Serve with Parmesan cheese.

REMIPE®
FOR
HANGOVER

This remipe is a good all round preventative and cure - before, during and immediately after drinking.

Cheese and pasta are good sources of amino acids that activate alcohol absorption and increase the speed at which your body processes alcohol.

Drink a glass of orange juice to replenish vitamin C that is lost due to the alcohol.

Steamed fish with lime, ginger and spinach

INGREDIENTS

serves 2

300 g   spinach, washed and drained (use pre-washed baby spinach to save time)
1   tablespoon lime juice
1   tablespoon extra-virgin olive oil
     salt and pepper to season
250 g   white fish fillets
1   lime zest
½   tablespoon ginger, finely grated
½   tablespoon sesame oil
     (substitute with olive oil if not available)

METHOD

Heat water in a large saucepan that will fit a steamer (later to cook fish) over medium heat.

Add spinach to water and cook for 2 minutes or until wilted and bright green. Transfer spinach to a plate without excess water. Mix with lime juice and oil. Season with salt and pepper. Set aside until the fish is ready.

Place the fish on a plate that will fit into the steamer and sprinkle with lime zest and ginger.

Steam for about 10 minutes or until the fish is cooked. Take care not to overcook the fish.

Season with salt and pepper.

Serve fish with spinach and drizzle sesame oil on top.

REMIPE® FOR HEADACHE

It is critical to eat a well-balanced diet with plenty of fresh, non-processed foods to prevent and cure migraines and headaches.

This includes a variety of grains, vegetables and fruits.

Foods that are renowned to be effective in curing headaches are ginger, fish, foods rich in calcium such as spinach, broccoli, kale and foods rich in magnesium such as spinach, oatmeal, wheat and garlic.

Turkey and cottage cheese pasta salad

INGREDIENTS

serves 4

400 g	spiral pasta
400 g	turkey breast, diced into small cubes
2	tablespoons canola oil or oil spray
300 g	cottage cheese
200 g	grape tomatoes (cut into similar size as the turkey pieces if using bigger tomatoes)
4	tablespoons chopped basil leaves, plus some more leaves to garnish
	salt and pepper to season

Dressing
2	tablespoons lemon juice
4	tablespoons extra virgin olive oil

METHOD

Preheat oven grill to 180°C.

Place turkey on a lined baking tray and mix with oil (or spray oil). Bake for 5 minutes or until golden brown. Set aside to cool.

Cook pasta in salted boiling water for 8 minutes or until cooked al dente. Rinse in cold water and set aside.

Combine lemon juice and olive oil to make dressing. Add the oil mixture, tomatoes and chopped basil to the pasta and mix well.

Add turkey and cottage cheese to the pasta and toss gently to combine. Season with salt and pepper.

Garnish with basil leaves and serve.

REMIPE® FOR HEADACHE

Serotonin is a neurotransmitter and low serotonin levels have been linked to depression, lack of concentration, obesity, sleeplessness and migraines.

Your body doesn't get serotonin from foods, but makes serotonin from tryptophan. Tryptophan is an amino acid which is the precursor for your body to generate neurotransmitters.

Tryptophan-rich foods include bread, pasta, turkey, duck, chicken, wheat germ, granola and cottage cheese. Turkey and cottage cheese both rank highly on the list for tryptophan potency.

Avocado rice with coriander and green onions

INGREDIENTS

4   cups warm cooked rice
(see page 166 for cooking instruction)
2   medium-sized avocados, halved and deseeded
2   tablespoons lime juice
½   cup chopped coriander
4   tablespoons finely sliced green onions
salt and pepper to season

serves 4

METHOD

Mash avocados with a fork on a plate and add lime juice.

Place rice in a large bowl, add avocado mash, coriander and green onions and mix well.

Season with salt and pepper and serve.

Avocado provides beneficial fats to build the foundation for an energised day.

Avocado contains the monounsaturated fat which assists in increased blood circulation, which is essential for optimal brain functioning.

This remipe takes no time to prepare when you have leftover rice, making it a great choice for a busy working day dinner.

Cannellini bean dip with thyme

serves 4

INGREDIENTS

Dip
1   can cannellini beans, rinsed and drained
1 ½   tablespoons fresh thyme leaves
1   garlic clove, sliced
½   tablespoon lemon juice
2   tablespoons extra virgin olive oil
     salt and pepper to season

To Serve
1   carrot cut into chip size sticks
2   celery stems cut into chip size sticks

METHOD

Blend all dip ingredients in a food processor.

Serve with carrot and celery sticks.

RE**M**IPE®
FOR HIGH
BRAIN
PERFORMANCE

The brain uses about 20% of your carbohydrate intake and needs a consistent supply of it.

Beans are truly amazing – loaded with fibre, vitamins, minerals and protein. Beans provide a steady, slow release of glucose to your brain, which means energy all day without a sugar crash.

Garlic reduces bad cholesterol and strengthens your cardiovascular system along with exerting a protective antioxidant effect on the brain.

Crispy spinach with panko

INGREDIENTS

300 g	spinach, cleaned and roughly chopped (if you are using baby spinach leaves, there is no need to chop them)
200 g	ricotta, cottage or quark cheese
½	cup Parmesan cheese, grated
2	cloves garlic, finely chopped
½	teaspoon nutmeg
	salt and pepper to season

Topping

½	cup panko (Japanese bread crumbs)
2	tablespoons olive oil

METHOD

serves 2

Preheat oven to 180°C.

Place spinach in a saucepan and cook for 2 minutes or until it has slightly wilted. Drain and squeeze out the excess water.

Place the spinach and all other ingredients, except those for topping, into a baking dish and mix well.

Combine the topping ingredients in a bowl and spread the mixture on top of the spinach.

Bake for 15 minutes and then place under the grill for another 3-5 minutes to brown the topping.

Serve as a main or as a side dish.

REMIPE®
FOR HIGH
BRAIN
PERFORMANCE

This is another delicious way to eat spinach, the super vegetable.

Green leafy vegetables including spinach, kale, chard, romaine and rocket are high in iron.

Slightly 'less green' sources include beef, pork and lamb.

A deficiency in iron is linked to 'restless leg syndrome', fatigue, poor mood, foggy thinking and other cognition issues.

You can substitute spinach with Swiss chard or rocket for variety.

Dark chocolate and pomegranate snow over quark cheese

INGREDIENTS

serves 2

300 g	quark cheese
2	teaspoons icing sugar
30 g	dark chocolate with 70% cocoa, grated
½	pomegranate fruit, seeds separated

METHOD

Add icing sugar to quark cheese and mix well.

Sprinkle with the chocolate and pomegranate seeds.

* To separate pomegranate seeds from the shell, halve the fruit, hold one half with cut-side down. Tap the curvy side with the back of a wooden spoon. Seeds will come out like falling snow.

REMIPE® FOR HIGH BRAIN PERFORMANCE

This is an easy and decadent dessert remipe to help you become smarter without making you fat!

Dark chocolate has powerful antioxidant properties and contains several natural stimulants including caffeine.

Caffeine enhances focus and concentration and stimulates the production of the feel-good chemical, endorphin. Enjoy in moderation!

Pomegranate offers potent antioxidant benefits which protect the brain from the damage of free radicals.

Quark cheese gives you smooth and creamy richness with only 20% of the calories of full fat cream cheese.

Pan-fried fish with wilted spinach

INGREDIENTS

serves 2

Wilted spinach

1	tablespoon canola oil
15 g	butter
200 g	spinach, washed and drained
2	garlic cloves, chopped
½	teaspoon ground nutmeg
1	tablespoon lemon juice
	salt and pepper to season

Pan-fried fish

½	teaspoon turmeric powder
1	tablespoon plain flour
½	teaspoon salt
¼	teaspoon pepper
2	tablespoons canola oil
15 g	butter
250 g	white fish fillets

METHOD

Heat 1 tablespoon oil and 15 g butter in a frying pan over medium heat.

Add the spinach and garlic to the pan and cook for 1 minute or until spinach is wilted and turns bright green.

Sprinkle with nutmeg and lemon juice. Set aside and keep warm.

Combine turmeric powder, flour, salt and pepper on a plate. Coat fish fillets with the flour mixture.

Heat the 2 tablespoons canola oil and butter over medium heat in the same frying pan as you used for the spinach. Add the fish, skin-side down first, and cook for 1-2 minutes each side or until cooked through.

Serve the fish with wilted spinach.

REMIPE®
FOR LEG
CRAMPS

Dehydration is one of the main causes of leg cramps, so drink lots of water as the first line of action.

Potassium will help with muscle soreness and cramping, as it aids in regulating water in your body, and assists with muscle growth.

Bananas are great, but there are a variety of other excellent sources of potassium such as raisins, potatoes, spinach, fish and citrus fruits.

Turmeric is also known as a good cure for leg cramps.

Banana mash with raisins

INGREDIENTS

1   ripe banana
1   tablespoon raisins

serves 1

METHOD

Mash banana with a fork.

Sprinkle raisins on top of the banana mash.

* Serve banana with yoghurt to boost the potassium levels even further.

REMIPE® FOR LEG CRAMPS

High potassium levels will help lessen episodes of leg cramps.

Prepare this dessert to accompany the pan-fried fish and wilted spinach remipe for dinner and you'll boost your meal with extra potassium.

Foods which are easy to eat and rich in potassium include bananas, raisins, dried apricot, cantaloupe, dried figs, prunes, milk and yoghurt.

Potassium also has beneficial effects on the quality of your sleep.

Japanese soba noodles with salmon and asparagus

serves 4

INGREDIENTS

400 g	Soba noodles
4	litres water
2	tablespoons canola oil
20 g	butter
400 g	asparagus, cut into 2 cm lengths with the hard ends removed from the bottom,
350 g	salmon, cubed
½	cup Mirin (Japanese cooking wine)
3	tablespoons soy sauce
4	tablespoons dill leaves, chopped salt and pepper to season

METHOD

Cook the soba noodles in a large saucepan of boiling water as per packet instructions. Drain, rinse in cold water and set aside.

Add the oil and butter to a medium frying pan over medium heat.

Add asparagus and cook for 3 minutes or until it is bright green and soft. Set aside.

Add salmon, Mirin and soy sauce to the same pan and cook for 4 minutes or until gently cooked.

Combine soba noodles, asparagus, salmon and dill.

Season with salt and pepper.

REMIPE® FOR LOW MOOD AND DEPRESSION

We all have occasional low moods and we need to treat ourselves gently in these times.

If low moods become persistent for longer than a week, see your doctor to check if you are depressed.

Simple comfort food such as pasta is a good 'pick-me-up'. Slow sugar from pasta is the source of the feel-good chemical endorphin.

Omega 3 Essential Fatty Acid (EFA) from salmon regulates hormones and brain chemicals that control moods.

Asparagus is high in folic acid which is important for the proper functioning of the nervous system.

Brown rice with chicken and broccoli

INGREDIENTS

serves 4

2 cups brown rice, washed and drained
1 cup sweet rice, washed and drained
4 cups water
2 tablespoons canola oil
400 g chicken thigh fillets, cut into small pieces
2 medium-sized broccoli heads, cut into bite-sized pieces
2 cups cooked brown rice (see page 166 for cooking instruction)

Sauce
4 tablespoons soy sauce
2 tablespoons rice vinegar
½ teaspoon cayenne pepper
2 teaspoons sugar
2 teaspoons salt

METHOD

Bring the rice and water to the boil in a big saucepan over high heat.

Reduce heat to low and cook for another 30 minutes with a lid on.

Mix all sauce ingredients in a small bowl.

Heat a wok or large frying pan over medium heat, and add the oil and chicken. Cook for 2-3 minutes or until cooked through. Add the broccoli and sauce mixture and cook for 3-4 minutes or until the broccoli is tender.

Serve with brown rice.

REMIPE®
FOR LOW
MOOD AND
DEPRESSION

This is the Asian version of comforting, feel-good food equivalent to pasta.

Brown rice is not only nutritional but also pleasurable to eat when you mix with sweet rice (glutinous rice). It becomes sweeter and nuttier and the texture is enhanced.

Chicken is high in serotonin, a neurotransmitter that influences possitively brain cells related to mood.

Broccoli is high in folic acid, essential for the proper functioning of the nervous system.

Harissa tofu patties with sweet chilli sauce

INGREDIENTS

serves 2

150 g	hard tofu, mashed with a fork
2	tablespoons sunflower seeds
2	tablespoons sesame seeds, dry roasted and crushed
½	cup coriander, finely chopped including stems
2	tablespoons flour
2	eggs
1	long red chilli, de-seeded and finely chopped
2	cloves garlic, grated
½	teaspoon salt
½	teaspoon ground cumin
½	teaspoon ground coriander
1	tablespoon olive oil
2-4	tablespoons canola oil to cook the patties
2	tablespoons sweet chilli sauce

METHOD

Place all ingredients except the canola oil and sweet chilli sauce into a large bowl and combine well.

Heat the oil in a large frying pan over medium to high heat. Drop approximately 2 tablespoons of the patty mixture into the pan for each patty. Press and shape the patties using two spoons.

Cook the patties for 2-3 minutes on each side or until golden brown.

Serve with sweet chilli sauce.

REMIPE® FOR MENOPAUSE

Eat more phytoestrogens to make menopause a lot more bearable.

Phyto or plant oestrogens are natural chemicals found in foods which act in the body in a similar way to oestrogen and help keep our natural hormones in balance. They block the uptake of excess oestrogen and raise low levels when needed.

Increase your intake of phytoestrogens through soya milk, linseeds, tofu, pumpkins seeds, sesame seeds and sunflower seeds.

Puy lentil salad with goat's cheese and almonds

INGREDIENTS

200 g	green lentils
1	litre cold water
100 g	goat's cheese, crumbled into small pieces
50 g	slivered almonds
	Half a bunch parsley leaves, chopped

Dressing

1	tablespoon lemon juice
4	tablespoons extra virgin olive oil
1	teaspoon maple syrup
¼	teaspoon each of salt and pepper

serves 2

METHOD

Place lentils and water in a medium saucepan and bring to the boil.

Simmer lentils over medium heat for 20 minutes or until cooked to your liking. Drain and set aside.

Place all dressing ingredients into a large bowl and whisk well.

Add the lentils and mix well.

Serve with goat's cheese and almonds.

Sprinkle with the chopped parsley and serve.

REMIPE® FOR MENOPAUSE

Dry skin is one of the adverse symptoms of menopause.

Legumes, nuts and seeds such as lentils, pumpkin seeds, sunflower seeds and almonds contain vitamin E, zinc and calcium.

These nutrients and the oils in the nuts and seeds may help prevent dry skin and normalise hormone levels.

Spicy tofu with brown rice

serves 4

INGREDIENTS

2	tablespoons roasted sesame seed oil
½	teaspoon cayenne pepper
200 g	minced pork
3	tablespoons soy sauce
4	cloves garlic, finely chopped
2	tablespoons grated ginger
2	tablespoons sesame seeds, dry roasted and crushed
1	tablespoon brown sugar
400 g	medium-hard tofu, cut into small cubes
1	tablespoon corn starch
1 ½	cups chicken stock
4	tablespoons thinly sliced spring onion
3	cups cooked brown rice (see page 166 for cooking instructions)

METHOD

Heat the sesame seed oil in a medium saucepan over medium heat.

Add cayenne powder and cook for 1 minute (take care not to burn it).

Add pork, soy sauce, garlic, ginger, sesame seeds and sugar and cook for 3 minutes or until pork is cooked. Break pork mince with a wooden spoon to prevent lumps.

Gently add tofu and stir.

Dissolve corn starch in the stock. Add the stock to the tofu mixture and cook for 5 minutes.

Serve with brown rice and sprinkle spring onions on top.

* You can find ingredients such as roasted sesame seed oil, medium-hard tofu and dry-roasted and crushed sesame seeds at Asian grocery stores.

REMIPE® FOR MENOPAUSE

Soy, a significant ingredient in the traditional Japanese diet, is thought to be useful in preventing hot flushes in women.

In addition to soy and tofu products, women can combat hot flushes by eating foods rich in calcium, magnesium, vitamin E and fibre such as cold-pressed oils, green leafy vegetables, nuts (almonds are good) and whole grains.

If you think tofu tastes boring, this remipe will prove you wrong.

Turkey loaf with cottage cheese and sage

INGREDIENTS

3	eggs, boiled and peeled
3	tablespoons canola oil
400 g	onions, chopped
3	teaspoons dry sage
3	tablespoons Worcestershire sauce
1	teaspoon salt
½	teaspoon pepper
700 g	turkey breast, minced
250 g	cottage cheese
8	slices round pancetta

serves 10

METHOD

Preheat oven to 180°C.

Heat oil in a saucepan over medium heat and add onions, sage, Worcestershire sauce, salt and pepper. Cook for 4 minutes or until onions are soft.

Combine the onion mixture, turkey breast and cottage cheese in a bowl.

Line a loaf pan (approximately 20 cm x 10 cm x 7 cm) with pancetta slices. Place half the turkey mixture into the loaf pan and place eggs in a row in the middle. Cover the eggs with the remaining half of the turkey mixture. Cover the top with remaining pancetta slices.

Bake for 25 minutes and remove excess liquid. Bake for another 10 minutes until the top is golden brown.

Rest the turkey loaf for 10 minutes before removing it from the loaf pan.

Slice and serve with green salad.

Depression and irritability from menopause can be reduced significantly by eating sufficient protein foods that contain the amino acid tryptophan.

Tryptophan is found in turkey, cottage cheese, oats and legumes.

Our bodies manufacture the neurotransmitter, serotonin, by using tryptophan.

Serotonin helps moods and may help control sleep and appetite.

Cut and pack leftovers into individual servings and store in the freezer.

Beef steak and wilted spinach, followed by cheese

serves 2

INGREDIENTS

250 g rump or scotch fillet beef steak
1 tablespoon butter
1 tablespoon canola oil
150 g spinach
1 tablespoon lemon juice
   salt and pepper to season
2 pieces of Gruyere cheese or your favourite hard cheese

METHOD

Heat your frying pan to high heat. Add oil and butter to the pan.

When the butter melts, place steak in the pan. Turn the steak after one minute for medium rare*.

Cover your steak with foil and set aside.

Add spinach to the same pan and toss gently. Turn the heat off as soon as the spinach wilts. Sprinkle the lemon juice over the spinach.

Season with salt and pepper.

Serve the steak and spinach, followed by the cheese.

* If you like your steak medium, leave for another minute. If you prefer it well done, leave for another two minutes.

REMIPE®
FOR
MENSTRUATING
OR POSTNATAL
WOMEN

Feeling low during your period? Or are you the loving man who wonders what you can do for your woman who's feeling blue?

Preparing a simple, nutritious and delicious meal for yourself or your beloved woman will make you feel better from the moment you are in action.

This remipe will supply you with plenty of iron from the beef and spinach, and B12 from the cheese. These are essential to build up your blood and elevate your mood.

Seared beef with miso flavoured seaweed

INGREDIENTS

serves 2

30 g	dried seaweed (wakame)
1	tablespoon sesame oil to cook beef
200 g	beef, cut into thin strips
	salt and pepper to season the beef
½	tablespoon miso paste
½	cup Mirin (Japanese cooking wine)
½	cup water
1	tablespoon sesame oil for the seaweed

METHOD

Soak dried seaweed in cold water for 10 minutes and then use scissors to roughly cut the seaweed into shorter strips. Rinse and drain.

Heat your frying pan to high heat. Sear the beef with salt, pepper and sesame oil for two minutes or until golden brown. Set aside.

Dissolve the miso paste in Mirin or white wine.

Add Mirin and water to the pan you used to cook the beef and bring to boil.

Add seaweed and cook for 5 minutes, stirring, until seaweed is soft and absorbs most of the water.

Turn off the heat and add sesame oil.

Serve the beef on a bed of seaweed.

REMIPE®
FOR
MENSTRUATING
OR POSTNATAL
WOMEN

Coastal Asian countries such as Japan and Korea have relied on seaweed as a staple food in their diet for centuries due to its high mineral and vitamin content, with near-zero calorie count.

Seaweed is known for its highly therapeutic attributes such as allergy relief, as a cancer fighter and as a fat buster. Its nutritional value is exceptionally high.

This remipe aims to aid in re-supplying iron and B12 that are essential for building blood by using seaweed, beef (high iron content) and miso (high in B12 from the fermentation process).

Chicken, carrot and quinoa salad

serves 4

INGREDIENTS

1	cup quinoa, rinsed and drained
2	cups water
400 g	chicken thigh fillets, cut into bite-sized pieces
2	tablespoons canola oil or oil spray
2	teaspoons ground cumin
2	tablespoons lemon juice
3	tablespoons extra virgin olive oil
300 g	carrots, grated
3	tablespoons chopped parsley
	salt and pepper to season

METHOD

Preheat oven to 180°C and turn on the top grill function.

Place quinoa and water in a saucepan and bring to the boil.

Reduce heat to low and simmer with the lid on for 6 minutes or until most of the liquid is absorbed. Set aside.

Place chicken on a lined baking tray and mix with oil. Bake for 6 minutes or until cooked brown.

In a salad bowl, whisk ground cumin, lemon juice and olive oil.

Add the quinoa, chicken, carrots and parsley and mix well with the dressing.

REMIPE® FOR MUSCULAR STRENGTH

Meat and poultry provide you with high amounts of essential nutrients including B group vitamins and iron, plus more protein per serving than most of other foods.

Whole grains contain important vitamins, minerals and large amounts of dietary fibre.

Whole grains provide the fuel to muscles, which allowes them to grow and function properly.

Nutrient-rich whole grains include whole wheat, bulgar, barley, spelt, quinoa, popcorn, wild rice and long-grain brown rice.

Fried eggs with rosemary and borlotti beans

serves 2

INGREDIENTS

1	tablespoon canola oil
20 g	butter
1	can borlotti beans, rinsed and drained
2	sprigs rosemary, leaves removed (or you can use 1 teaspoon dried rosemary)
2	cloves garlic, chopped
	salt and pepper to season
4	eggs

METHOD

Heat 1 tablespoon of oil and butter in a frying pan over medium heat.

Add rosemary and garlic and cook for 1 minute. Add beans and cook for another minute. Set aside.

Heat remaining oil in the same frying pan over medium heat.

Break eggs into the pan and cook to your liking.

Season with salt and pepper.

Serve eggs with beans.

REMIPE® FOR MUSCULAR STRENGTH

This remipe provides quality protein to build strong muscles.

Egg protein is of such high quality that it is often used as the standard by which other proteins are measured.

Egg protein contains all the essential amino acids. These are the building blocks of protein which the body needs but cannot make - in a pattern that very closely matches the pattern the body needs.

Beans provide your body with fibre, complex carbohydrates and protein.

Use this remipe as your power breakfast. It takes little time to prepare this breakfast.

Salmon and spinach tart with ricotta cheese

INGREDIENTS

serves 4

½ tablespoon canola oil or oil spray to brush on the tart case (22 cm diameter)
2 sheets of ready-rolled frozen shortcrust pastry, softened
300 g baby spinach
200 g salmon fillet, cut into small cubes
250 g ricotta cheese
2 eggs
2 tablespoons grated Parmesan cheese, plus 1 tablespoon extra to sprinkle on top salt and pepper to season

METHOD

Preheat oven to 180°C.

Spray or brush oil over the tart case and line the case with pastry. Make holes in the base with a fork and blind bake for 10 minutes.

Meanwhile, cook the spinach in a saucepan over medium heat for 3 minutes or until wilted. Rinse in cold water and squeeze the excess water from the spinach.

Combine the ricotta cheese, eggs and 2 tablespoons of Parmesan cheese in a bowl.

Place salmon and spinach on the pastry. Pour the ricotta cheese mixture into the tart pastry and smooth the surface with the back of a spoon. Sprinkle the remaining cheese on top.

Bake for 25 minutes or until the top is golden brown.

RE**M**IPE®
FOR
MUSCULAR
STRENGTH

Salmon is an excellent source of protein and high in Omega-3 fatty acids which help your body function optimally.

Spinach is high in vitamins A and C as well as folate. It's a good source of fibre and may also help reduce the risk of several diseases such as cancer and age-related macular degeneration.

You will definitely be stronger by eating these two super foods together.

Ginger and mint tea

INGREDIENTS

3 cm	piece ginger, sliced thinly
2	sprigs mint, leaves only
800 ml	water

METHOD

serves 5

Place the ginger and mint in a heatproof jug or saucepan.

Boil water and pour over the ginger and mint.

Steep for 5 minutes and drink as often as you can.

REMIPE® FOR NAUSEA AND VOMITING

Dehydration is often the most common cause of nausea and vomiting.

Make sure that you drink enough liquids. Especially clear liquids such as water will help keep you hydrated.

Mint and ginger are both known to have a soothing effect on an upset stomach.

Ginger poached chicken with potato mash

INGREDIENTS

250 g	chicken breast fillets, halved horizontally to make thin slices
2 cm	piece ginger, thinly sliced
300 g	potatoes, peeled and cut into small chunks
1	litre water

METHOD

serves 2

If you have a steamer that fits on top of your saucepan, cook the chicken in the simmering water and steam the potatoes in the steamer at the same time. Remove the chicken after the first 5 minutes of cooking and continue to cook potatoes for further 7 minutes or until soft.

Otherwise, cook the chicken and potatoes separately as follows:

Pour water with ginger in a saucepan and bring to the boil. Place potatoes in a steamer and cook potatoes for 12 minutes over medium heat or until soft. Mash the potatoes with a fork using some of the ginger water. Set aside and keep warm.

Bring the ginger water (which was used for cooking the potatoes) to the boil again and add the chicken. Simmer on medium heat for 5 minutes or until cooked.

Serve the chicken with the potato mash.

REMIPE®
FOR
NAUSEA
AND
VOMITING

Avoid spicy, sweet or high-fat foods.

The 'BRAT' diet, consisting of bananas, rice, apple sauce, and toast, includes bland foods that help to absorb stomach acids and ease nausea and vomiting.

Try this remipe after you can handle the BRAT diet comfortably.

Steam potatoes rather than boiling in order to keep nutrient levels at their maximum.

Chicken, chickpea and pistachio salad

serves 4

INGREDIENTS

1	tablespoon canola oil
300 g	chicken breast fillets, cut into small cubes
250 g	cos lettuce, washed and cut into bite-sized pieces
1	can chickpeas, rinsed and drained
½	cup unsalted pistachio nuts, shelled

Dressing

½	tablespoon Dijon mustard
1	tablespoon white balsamic vinegar
4	tablespoons extra virgin olive oil
¼	teaspoon salt
¼	teaspoon pepper

METHOD

Heat the oil in a medium frying pan over medium/high heat. Add the chicken and cook for 4 minutes or until golden brown. Set aside.

Place all dressing ingredients in a jar and shake well.

Place cos lettuce, chicken, chickpeas, pistachio nuts and the dressing in a salad bowl. Combine well.

Serve the salad with slices of crusty multi-grain bread.

RE**M**IPE®
FOR PRE-MENSTRUAL SYNDROME (PMS)

Keeping vitamin B6 levels high in your body will help reduce water retention, breast tenderness, irritability and symptoms of depression.

Vitamin B6 plays a vital role in synthesising certain brain chemicals that control your mood and behaviour.

Foods rich in vitamin B6 include whole grains, chickpeas, lean beef, white potatoes with skin on, bananas, chicken breast and unsalted pistachio nuts.

Miso braised salmon and spinach with brown rice

INGREDIENTS

serves 2

250 g	spinach, washed, drained and roughly chopped
1	tablespoon Japanese brown miso paste
2	tablespoons soy sauce
4	tablespoons Mirin (Japanese cooking wine)
1	tablespoon brown sugar
250 g	salmon fillets
1 ½	cups cooked brown rice (see page 166 for cooking instructions)

METHOD

Heat a medium saucepan over medium heat and add spinach.

Cook until wilted and dark green.

Set aside and retain the cooking water from the spinach in your pan.

Add miso, soy sauce, Mirin and brown sugar to the same pan. Bring to the boil and reduce heat to low.

Add the salmon and cook for 2 minutes. Turn salmon over and cook for another 2 minutes.

Place salmon, spinach and brown rice on a place. Drizzle miso sauce on top and serve.

REMIPE®
FOR PRE-MENSTRUAL SYNDROME (PMS)

Magnesium reduces water retention and PMS symptoms. It also helps to regulate serotonin that balances mood in the brain.

Magnesium-rich food sources include peanut butter, brown rice and whole-grain bread. Other foods which also help knock out PMS are beans, sunflower seeds, spinach, wild salmon and cashews.

Calcium is also known to lessen symptoms of PMS, including irritability.

Broccoli, kale and white beans are rich in calcium as well as dairy products such as milk, cheese and yoghurt.

Carrot soup with turmeric

INGREDIENTS

2	tablespoons canola oil
1	tablespoon butter
3	cloves garlic, chopped
1	large onion, finely chopped
1	bunch of coriander stems, finely chopped (set aside the leaves to add to the soup at the end)
3	teaspoons turmeric powder
500 g	carrots, finely chopped
400 ml	water
500 ml	chicken stock
2	tablespoons lemon juice
	coriander leaves, finely chopped
	salt to season

serves 4

METHOD

Place the oil and butter in a medium sized saucepan over medium heat.

Add the garlic, onion, coriander stems and turmeric powder to the pan and cook for 2 minutes or until soft.

Add carrots and cook for a further 5 minutes or until they're soft.

Add water and chicken stock and increase the heat to bring to the boil. Then reduce the heat to low and simmer for 10 minutes. Turn the heat off.

Blend the soup to a smooth texture (using a Bamix is convenient).

Add lemon juice and coriander leaves.

* It will save time and effort, if you use a food processor to chop vegetables.

REM**I**PE®
FOR
SORE
THROAT

This remipe is based on the first rule of treating a sore throat: keep your throat well hydrated. Drinking this mild soup will soothe your painful throat.

A sore throat is usually caused by a viral infection. Therefore this remipe includes ingredients such as garlic and onion which are good to treat a cold.

Turmeric is a terrific anti-inflammatory, known as a magic cure for a sore throat. Avoid pepper not to irritate your throat.

Warm honey, lemon and ginger tea

serves 1

INGREDIENTS

250 ml	boiled water
1	tablespoon honey
2	tablespoons freshly squeezed lemon juice
1 cm	piece of ginger, finely sliced

METHOD

Place honey, lemon juice and ginger in a mug.

Pour hot water in the mug and steep for 1 minute before serving.

* If you drink this tea late in the evening, skip the lemon juice, as vitamin C may hinder your sleep. Warm water and honey will soothe your throat and help you get a good night's sleep.

REMIPE®
FOR
SORE
THROAT

A sore throat often develops at the onset of a cold.

If you are successful in managing a sore throat successfully at the beginning, you might be lucky enough to avoid a full bout of a cold.

This drink is my regular tea (5-6 times a day), when I have a sore throat.

It is even more effective if you gargle 3-4 times per day with warm salted water.

Brown rice mixed with sweet rice

INGREDIENTS

serves 4

1   cup brown rice, rinsed and drained
    (medium grain or Basmati)
½   cup sweet rice, rinsed and drained
3   cups water

METHOD

Place brown rice, sweet rice and water in a medium saucepan over high heat. Bring it to the boil. This will take about 5 minutes.

Reduce heat to low and simmer with the lid on for 20 - 25 minutes or until soft.

Stir cooked rice with a spatula to release steam from the inside.

You can freeze leftover rice in serving portions to use later.

* When you cook brown rice with sweet rice, the texture is wonderfully soft and pleasant to eat.

A TASTY WAY TO ENJOY BROWN RICE

Brown rice is the 'unrefined' version of white rice with the side hull and bran intact.

The side hulls and brans provide 'natural wholeness' to the grain and are rich in proteins, thiamine, calcium, magnesium, fibre and potassium.

If you are trying to lose weight, or suffer from diabetes, brown rice is a healthy choice as its low glycaemic index rating helps to reduce insulin spikes.

Brown rice is rich in selenium which reduces the risk for developing serious illnesses such as cancer, heart disease and arthritis.

Just like all other types of rice, sweet rice does not contain dietary gluten. Sweet rice is also called sticky or glutinous rice due to its glue-like texture. Hence it is safe to use sweet rice for gluten-free diets.

References

Stanton, Dr Rosemary. Foods that harm, foods that heal
Copyright © 1997 The Readers Digest Association, Inc.

Carper, Jean. Food, your miracle medicine
Copyright © 1993 by Jean Carper. HarperCollins Publishers

USDA Nutrient Database for Standard Reference:
http://ndb.nal.usda.gov

Nutrition Australia: http://www.nutritionaustralia.org/

American Cancer Society: http://www.cancer.org.au/preventing-cancer/nutrition-andphysical-activity/
food-and-nutrition.html

Dr JD Decuypere, DC: http://www.health-alternatives.com/vegetables-nutrition-chart.html

Britannica:
http://www.britannica. com/EBchecked/topic/422916/nutritional-disease

'Disease prevention through diet and nutrition':
http://www.medicinenet.com/prevention/article.htm

Kotz, C. M.: In vitro antibacterial effect of yogurt on Escherichia coli. Digestive Diseases and Science
1990:35(5):630-37

'Nutrition during illness':
http://www.saga.co.uk/health/healthy-eating/nutrition-duringillness.aspx

Radnitz, C.L.: Food-triggered migraine: a critical review. Annals of Behavioural Medicine 1990; 12(2):51-65

Academy of Nutrition and Dietetics: http://www.eatright.org

Saketkhoo, K. : Effects of drinking hot water, cold water and chicken soup on nasal mucus velocity
and nasal airflow resistance. Chest 1978; 74:408-10

Lau, B. H.S.: Garlic compounds modulate macrophage and T-lymphocyte functions. Molecular
Biotherapy 1991; 3:103-7

Index

Index (By Meal Type)

Index (By Meal Type)

Index (By Key Ingredients)

Index (By Key Ingredients)

Index (By Key Ingredients)

Index (By Key Ingredients)

Index (By Key Ingredients)

Index (By Key Ingredients)

Index (By Health and Nutrition Terms)

Index (By Health and Nutrition Terms)

Index (By Health and Nutrition Terms)